# RELEVANT INTERESTS

By

# Cecelia Frances Page

iUniverse, Inc.
New York   Bloomington

# Relevant Interests

*iUniverse books may be ordered through booksellers or by contacting:*

*iUniverse*
*1663 Liberty Drive*
*Bloomington, IN 47403*
*www.iuniverse.com*
*1-800-Authors (1-800-288-4677)*

*ISBN: 978-1-4401-4706-7 (pbk)*
*ISBN: 9781--4401-4707-4 (ebk)*

*Printed in the United States of America*

*iUniverse rev. date: 6/15/2009*

# Contents

# CONTENTS

# PREFACE

<u>RELEVANT INTERESTS</u> is an exciting, dynamic book of fifty-six short stories and articles about a wide variety of topics and interests. Exciting topics include Revelations That Will Astound You!, Shamballa, The Value Of Crystals, Lemurian and Atlantean Temples and Seven Root Races On Earth. More fascinating topics are Ocean Mysteries, Butterflies, Umbrellas And Parasols, Stained Glass Objects, The Etheric Universe, Chemical And Alchemical Affinity and A True Story, Golden Days, Avatars Exist, Santa Claus, Porcelain Paraphernalia, Frame Your Photos and Paintings, Creekside Adventures and Japanese Baths are stimulating topics.

Russian Village Life, Edgar Cayce Insights, Avoid Accidents, Into The Light, Effects Of Painkillers, Echoes From the Past, Use Of VCRs And DVD Players, Lighthouses Beacon, Old Victorian Houses, Experiencing Diabetes, Seashore Painting, Games And Puzzles, Up In The Attic, Scavengers Exist and Ballroom Dancing are more worthwhile topics. Keeping A Current Address Book, The Charity Dinner, Llamas From South America, Wearing Dark Glasses, Theogenesis Revealed, Elephants Still Live, My High School P.E. Teachers, Pencils

And Pens, The Forest Dwellers, A Campfire Story, Office Chatter, Movie and Stageplay Goers and Electricity Counts are diverse and dynamic topics.

Candlelight Services, The Garden Party, Beverly Sills, A Famous Opera Star, The Importance of Early Childhood Education, Parapsychology, Toronto, A Cosmopolitan City, The Louvre In Paris, France, Unlocking the Genetic Code and The Science Of Dreams will enlighten you.

# About The Author

Cecelia Frances Page has published five, original screenplays and three, original, poetry books. The original screenplays are entitled <u>Walking in the Light</u>, <u>Flashbacks</u>, <u>Celestial Connections I and II</u> and <u>Adventures in Lemuria I and II</u>. The three, original, poetry books are entitled <u>Cosmic Dimensions</u>, <u>Vivid Impressions</u> and <u>Significant Introspections</u>. Cecelia Frances Page has written over five hundred, original poems. Several of her poems are published in <u>The World's Best Poems of 2004 and 2005</u>.

Cecelia has been writing since the age of 19. She has written 43 books. Some of her books published by iUniverse are entitled: <u>Westward Pursuit</u>, <u>Opportune Times</u>, <u>Imagine If...</u>, <u>Fortunately</u>, <u>Mystical Realities</u>, <u>Magnificent Celestial Journeys</u>, <u>Extraordinary Encounters</u>, <u>Brilliant Candor</u>, <u>Expand Your Awareness</u>, <u>Seek Enlightenment Within</u>, <u>Vivid Memories of Halcyon</u>, <u>Awaken to Spiritual Illumination</u>, <u>Adventures on Ancient Continents</u>, <u>Pathways to Spiritual Realization</u>, <u>Celestial Connections</u>, <u>Phenomenal Experiences</u>, <u>Celestial Beings from Outer Space</u>, <u>Awesome Episodes</u>, <u>Incredible Times</u>, <u>Interpretations of Life</u>, <u>New Perspectives</u>, <u>Tremendous Moments</u>, <u>Amazing Stories and Articles</u>, <u>Horizons Beyond</u>, <u>Fascinating Topics</u>, <u>Certain People</u>

Make A Difference, Adventurous Experiences, The Future Age Beyond The New Age Movement, Power of Creative and Worthwhile Living, Extraterrestrial Civilizations on Earth, Relevant Interests, Remarkable World Travels, Impressionable Occurrences and more.

Cecelia Frances Page has a B.A. and M.A. in Education with a focus in English, Speech and Psychology. Cecelia is an excellent pianist. She is a piano and voice teacher, author, educator, philosopher, photographer and artist. Cecelia believes that creative abilities and talents can be achieved. Cecelia Frances Page continues to write more, worthwhile books to inspire her readers.

# ONE

## *REVELATIONS THAT WILL ASTOUND YOU!*

The Earth is humanity's home and dwelling place. Six billion people are affected by Earth changes, climates and human behavior. The Earth was created approximately four-and-a-half billion years ago.

The Earth exploded from the Sun. It was a fireball in the beginning. Gradually the Earth hardened. Comets and meteorites crashed to Earth for over a billion years. The Earth kept changing. Finally water emerged all over the surface of the Earth.

Plants such as algae and plankton began growing in the water which began in the oceans. Then fish began to multiply. They ate plankton and algae to survive. It is said fish eventually evolved into mermaids and mermen.

As animals came on Earth they changed the environment. For instance, dinosaurs ate large volumes of vegetables and foliage. They roamed around from one group of trees and foliage to other groups of foliage. They ate up a great quantity of foliage.

More plants had to grow so that large animals would have enough to eat. Rain poured down and this helped seeds to spread and grow into tropical plants with very large leaves. The abundance of tropical plants was necessary so life could go on.

The dinosaur kingdom flourished on Earth for millions of years. Tropical climates existed, so Earth was a luscious, green covered environment. It appeared that life on Earth would go on the same way. Then one day approximately 65 million years ago a sudden, dramatic change took place on Earth.

Cataclysms occurred when the Earth was bombarded with a very large comet which caused extreme dust storms. The sky became dark and the sun was obscured from the Earth's surface. The Earth dried up, cracked and caused life on Earth to die.

Cataclysms caused plants to burn up. Water disappeared and there was no food for the dinosaurs to eat. They fell in deep cracks and collapsed on the desolate, parched ground and literally died and perished.

There were no human beings on Earth during the cataclysms that occurred 65 million years ago. The dinosaurs became extinct. They were buried in the layers of sediment and soil. Only a few descendant species remained on Earth. The blue lizard still exists on the Galapagos Islands. It is a big, lizard-like creature that is a descendant of the dinosaurs.

Life changed considerably after the sudden, unexpected calamity 65 million years ago. There were no plants and water for quite some time. Finally the dust storms blew away. It began to rain again. The soil on the Earth's surface provided nutrients. New plants began to grow. Then new, smaller animals began to live on Earth.

During ancient times there have been different millenniums which were cycles of time. Each millennium was a period of evolution. Animal life began to evolve. Mammals, reptiles and amphibians have dwelled on Earth.

After several million years human beings came to Earth. Ancient continents of Lumania, Lemuria, Atlantis, etc, formed. Human beings lived in ancient civilizations. Human beings may have come from other planets. Early, ancient parchments in Egypt, India and Persia describe light-skinned, blonde and red haired people who lived in Lemuria and then in Atlantis. Our ancient ancestors evolved and developed technology. They were adept in their religious viewpoints.

Before the fall of both Lemuria and Atlantis soothsayers and priests predicted the destruction of these large continents. Both Lemuria and Atlantis fell into the ocean. Some of the people escaped this tragedy by migrating to other continents.

Lemurians in the land of Mu remained in the Hawaiian Islands, which was the remainder of Mu or Lemuria. Some other Lemurians migrated to Mount Shasta in California. They lived inside of Mount Shasta. They continued with their Lemurian, ancient beliefs and religion.

Lemuria and Atlantis were destroyed because of misuse of the sacred fire. Priests and priestesses foresaw the fall of these continents. The priests and priestesses predicted the cataclysms and the sudden fall of these large continents. Therefore, a certain number of the descendants were saved when they migrated to other places. Descendants of early Lemurians and Atlanteans still exist on Earth. Much has been lost and forgotten about Lemuria and Atlantis.

Original accountings were destroyed about the fall of Lemuria and Atlantis because these continents disappeared in the ocean never to be seen again. In recent times within the last one hundred years theosophists such as Madame Helena Blavatsky revealed ancient knowledge that she received in messages from masters and adepts.

Madame Helena Blavatsky wrote about Lemuria and Atlantis in The Secret Doctrine and Isis Unveiled. She wrote over 500 pages in these books to reveal the cause of the fall of these ancient continents. The Lemurians were a spiritual race on Earth. However, they became technical and they developed an advanced technology. Lemurians eventually learned to use laser energy. Some laser energy was useful for medical reasons. Laser beams were used for surgery. Eventually laser energy was used in weapons. This destructive use of laser energy caused Lemuria to fall.

Atlanteans developed technology as they progressed. Today modern civilizations have developed sophisticated technology. Laser equipment is used for medical purposes. Even eye surgery is successful today. Yet, nuclear weapons have been created and used just as they were used in Atlantis.

We should review ancient history and try to learn from the past mistakes made in ancient civilizations such as Atlantis and Lemuria.

Bible predictions have been clarified in the Old Testament. Noah was warned about the flood in Sodom and Gomorrah. The Jews were told to flee from Egypt to the Promised Land in Israel. They were warned by Moses and hundreds of years later by Jesus to live by the Golden Rule and brotherhood. Moses warned the Jews to promote peace and to avoid war with other nations. The Jews have fought with other Middle Eastern people over land and resources. This had caused a lot of friction between the Jews and other Middle Eastern countries.

Prophets in the Bible have prophesized about the future karma of the civilization they lived in. Daniel warned his civilization to get along with other peoples who lived in the surrounding region. Daniel was devoted to God. He was persecuted because he believed in the power of God and in God's will. He proved to the nonbelievers that God exists when he tamed lions in a den. His life was saved because the lions did not attack him!

Ezekiel went up in a blazing chariot into the heavens. He ascended into the heavens to be with God. The description of his chariot was spectacular. He described a modular spacecraft with four legs. Blazing lights could be seen in the spacecraft. Ezekiel sat in a seat in the center of the spacecraft. He was wearing a space outfit and space helmet. This suggests that Ezekiel traveled in space and came to Earth. He then went back into space into celestial heaven.

Edgar Cayce was capable of revealing psychic visions in the 19th Century when he was alive. He was a "sleeping prophet." He predicted World War I, II, the Vietnam War and the assassination of John F. Kennedy, America's 36th President. Cayce had visions of Lemuria as well. It was revealed to Cayce that Lemuria was destroyed in a cataclysm. He also revealed many cases of reincarnation which amazed other people. Edgar Cayce was one of the first to expose reincarnation as real. Reincarnation means rebirth of a soul in a new body. "We have many embodiments on Earth," Edgar Cayce said. "We are responsible for everything we do in each incarnation."

Nostradamos was a seeing prophet from France in the 18th Century. He made accurate predictions about what would happen to royalty in France. He also had visions of future events and wars. He foresaw atomic explosions that would occur. He warned people who he thought were in danger. He wanted his visions to be accepted.

Psychics and prophets have revealed their revelations and visions to those around them to help them to make better decisions. They hoped what they revealed to others would bring them insight and understanding regarding future happenings and events. Different prophets and psychics have predicted cataclysms, wars and other catastrophes.

2012 A.D. marks the end of the Mayan Calendar. The Mayans are extinct. They were aware of the end of their calendar before they disappeared. Quetcolcoatle, a Mayan god, helped to write the calendar. He said he would return someday.

We can make a difference as world citizens by making an effort to take care of our environment. We can promote peaceful lifestyles. We can be kind, loving and helpful to others around us. As world citizens we can promote good will, harmony and we can live by the Golden Rule. We are part of a Cosmic Plan in the Universe. God cares about the future of the world's humanity.

# TWO

## *SHAMBALLA*

Shamballa is in the Himalayan Mountains in Tibet. Shamballa is a dwelling place with flat roofed, thick walled, white, stucco walls. Small windows exist in the front of the dwellings. One dwelling is built on top of another dwelling.

Shamballa has tunnels that lead into the Himalayan Mountains. Sacred, religious treasures are kept in the secret tunnels. Religious chanting is practiced in religious rooms where Buddhist members gather. They wear beautiful gowns with bright colors and they wear elaborate hats that distinguish them as participating in ceremonies.

The lamas of Tibet are Buddhists. They live by an eightfold path of renunciation, purification, right concentration, right action, right occupation, right association, right morals and behavior. The lamas live a strict life of religious expectations. They live in the Himalayan Mountains away from worldly ways and habits.

The lamas follow the Dali Lama. They left Tibet and followed their leader, the Dali Lama into India when Chinese

Communists came into Tibet to invade the religious groups that existed there. The Dali Lama left Tibet in 1959. He has been out of Tibet approximately 50 years. He continues to practice Buddhism in India.

Chinese Communists destroyed the dwellings and Buddhist Monasteries in 1959. Many Tibetans have been killed by the Chinese Communists. The Tibetans, who survived Communist invasions, had to conform to Chinese Communist policies and expectations. Many of them lost economic protection. They suffered and have lived in poverty.

The Dali Lama prays for the Tibetan people. He hopes Tibetans will prosper and live in peace again.

# THREE

## *THE VALUE OF CRYSTALS*

Crystals exist inside the Earth. They are created deep in rocks and sediment. Crystals are very refined, precious stones. The crystals shine once they are polished. Crystals are very pretty. Clear crystals shine brightly when exposed to sunlight. They sparkle with reflections of multiple colors.

Geometric designs reflect from within unusual crystals. Rays of light blaze outward sending light and amazing colors into the atmosphere.

Crystals are more evolved minerals. They amplify electrical energy. Crystals are constantly growing because they are alive. Atlanteans powered their cities with crystal energy. Laser energy was used to carve crystals. Sound frequencies were also used to create extremely complex, mathematical and geometrical, faceted patterns. Crystal energy was used to power aircraft, spacecraft and appliances. Atlanteans transmitted crystal energy from transmitting towers.

Atlanteans didn't need to use oil and gasoline because they used crystal energies instead. Crystal energy was transmitted through the Earth's atmosphere. Crystals were much bigger than houses.

We do not have enormous crystals today. However, crystals can be found deep in the Earth. If humanity used crystals today they would not need to use oil and gasoline. Air and water pollution would disappear on Earth if crystal energy was used today.

# FOUR

## *LEMURIAN AND ATLANTEAN TEMPLES*

Ancient continents which were called Lemuria and Atlantis existed on our planet, Earth millions of years ago. Advanced civilizations dwelled on these continents. Many of them worshipped sun gods and nature spirits.

Lemurians built large, circular temples with columns and pillars. Temples had many stairways as well as columns and archways that look down to the water. There were big, gold doors and a big, black, marble floor. Altars were portals with passageways. Crystals were in rings. The crystals were ten of twelve feet high.

Lemurian priests and priestesses chanted as them moved around the center of the temple. A crystal flame was blazing at the center at an altar.

Lemurian priests and priestesses chanted frequently to God in the Great Central Sun. They maintained flames of God energy. Priests and priestesses protected Lemuria. They protected the Earth with their powerful chants.

Lemurian priests and priestesses were very spiritual. They

had extrasensory perception. They had mental telepathy and telekinetic abilities. Lemurians came into their temples in different locations. For thousands of years Lemurians sent light rays from their inner, spiritual bodies into the astral and physical Earth to maintain balance, equilibrium, unity and purification on Earth.

Atlanteans built beautiful sun god temples on the continent of Atlantis. Atlantean priests and priestesses chanted at the altars in their great temples. They also were able to protect Atlantis and the Earth by praying to God. Atlantean gods have fohatic power to amplify crystal energy to produce balance, good climates and weather. They were able to stop hurricanes, typhoons, tidal waves, floods and fires.

Eventually Atlanteans were endangered on Atlantis because they misused the sacred energy and fire of God. They produced laser weapons and bombs which were very destructive. Atlantis finally fell into the ocean because of upheavals, cataclysms and sudden earthquakes caused from misqualified energy misused on a massive scale.

The Lemurians and Atlanteans were advanced for thousands of years. They lived by cosmic laws of love, unity, centralization and brotherhood. If they had not produced destructive weapons and they had used energy in a positive manner they would have had a better opportunity to survive.

# FIVE

## *SEVEN ROOT RACES ON EARTH*

There are seven root races of manifested life during each manvantara which is a great age or period of 432,000,000 solar years. There are seven sub-races in each root race and innumerable lesser tribal and family races in each sub-race. There are seven great ages and seven grand divisions of each great age and innumerable lesser cycles of that time within a single manvantara.

The first five root races have evolved on Earth already. The first root race existed in Lemuria. An ancient civilization of Lemurians dwelled on Lemuria. The second root race existed in Asia and Europe. The third root race was in Egypt, Sumeria, Babylon, Australia and Persia. The third and fourth root races were in Europe and America.

Presently the fifth root race is evolving in Europe and America. The sixth root race will dwell on a new continent or renewed continent. This continent will emerge from the depths of the ocean to become a new Garden of Eden for the home of the new race.

The present human race possesses the five active, sense organs. The sixth sub-race will possess six fully developed sense organs and the seventh sub-race will possess a synthetic sense organ which will combine the qualities of the six sense organs together with the seventh. The present atrophied pineal gland will be more active in the sixth sub-race and will be the organ through which the Kundalini force will function.

There are noticeable changes taking place in many of the children in the present time. Such changes as are occurring on the children and in some older people appear to the extensions of the present powers of sight and hearing as they are more of the nature of clairvoyance and clairaudience which are qualities developing in the humanity of the last races of the fifth sub-race and will be at the command of all people in the sixth sub-race.

The Kriyashakti force will function in the seventh race human body because of spiritual will. The seventh race will be a race of androgynes with masculine and feminine polarities. The pituitary bodies control the growth of the physical body.

Masters predict that the seventh root race may be a race of giants. The ductless glands and pineal gland are responsible for the dwarfing of the body in many instances and its action would seem to have been responsible for the short stature of even certain races at present.

According to occult science it is said that the teaching relating to the seventh root races and forty-nine sub-races which come into manifestation during a manvantara apply only to life on the Earth. Life on other planets may manifest under entirely different laws.

The sixth root race will be more evolved on Earth. They

may be able to bring reliable peace and harmony on Earth. The seventh root race will continue to protect the Earth. Perhaps cataclysms, earthquakes and floods will be controlled. These more spiritual races will restore our planet, Earth.

# SIX

## *OCEAN MYSTERIES*

Ocean mysteries exist on Earth. Nearly two-thirds of the Earth is covered with oceans. Many unknown, ocean floors are yet to be discovered. Oceanographers have discovered ancient ruins on the ocean floor near Greece, Japan, South America, Asia, Hawaii, North Pole and the Central Coast of California in Western America.

The Bermuda Triangle is another mystery in the ocean near Florida and Cuba. Planes and ships have sunk down into the ocean without warning. What causes then to sink in the ocean? Some magnetic force is in the ocean to cause this to happen. It is still a mystery how and why planes, ships and boats sink.

The Great Barrier Reef is still a mysterious location in the South Pacific Ocean. New sea life is yet to be discovered. Unknown fish, shell life, corals and other sea life has yet to be studied, examined as well as collected for further studies.

Many underwater ruins exist in the ocean. Ancient ruins have been discovered in the Mediterranean Sea and Aegean

Sea. Ancient cities with stone columns, streets and buildings still exist in the ocean. Ancient cities sank into the ocean millions of years ago. They have remained in the ocean all those years once they fell into the ocean.

The continent of Lemuria extended throughout the Pacific Ocean. Lemuria covered more than half of the ocean of Earth. Lemuria was in the Hawaiian Islands which were known to be where ancient Mu existed. Ancient, white races were living on Lemuria where California, Hawaii and other islands exist in the Pacific Ocean.

More ancient ruins are yet to be discovered in the oceans around the world. Even ancient, stone statues remain under the ocean. Many ancient temples exist under the ocean in sunken cities around the world. Ancient temples have stone floors, altars and columns. Some temples are rectangular and other temples are circular. Ancient civilizations build large, grand temples. Even the remaining ruins of temples are evidence of spectacular, architectural planning and building.

The Marianna Trench, near the Marianna Islands of Guan, Palau and Saipan, is the deepest location in the ocean. This deepest part of the ocean is still a mysterious area in the ocean. The Marianna Trench is so deep it is difficult to go into the darkest fathoms to locate unknown ocean species which live in this darkest location in the ocean.

Ocean species dwell in the Marianna Trench in ocean water thousands of feet deep. There is far less oxygen and no sunlight deep in the Marianna Trench. Yet, certain sea life is capable of living in dark water without light. These unknown species are still to be discovered and named. They live with very little oxygen. Their food is limited.

Antarctica near the South Pole has a deep ocean below

the ice. Oceanographers have been discovering sea life species such as sea anemones, spiders with long legs, sea slugs, sea urchins, iceopods and fish. More unknown sea life forms are being discovered in the ocean depth living in very ice-cold water.

More and more knowledge is being unveiled about ocean underwater environments, effects of ocean life on other sea life. Ocean temperatures, ocean currents, plankton, algae and ocean floor terrains affect the ocean environment.

The world's oceans should be protected, preserved and kept clean. We depend on ocean life to use for food and other resources. The world's people gather fish, sea plants, shellfish, octopi, oil and sea rocks, etc, from the ocean. There are more ocean mysteries to discover year by year. We should learn all we can about the world's oceans.

# SEVEN

## *BUTTERFLIES*

Butterflies are very beautiful. They are very colorful and their wings flutter as they fly in the air. Well known butterflies are monarchs, yellow winged and white butterflies. Some butterflies are purple-gold, black, black and white and multicolored.

Butterflies have their own seasons. They generally go through a cocoon stage before they emerge as full-fledged butterflies. Butterflies have a cycle of months which they live. They dwell in forests and fly around trees. They land in tree branches and on plants.

Butterflies are classified as Lepideptera. Butterflies are active during the daytime. They are a large group of insects. They have sucking mouth parts. They have slender bodies with rope-like knobs and four broad, usually brightly colored, membranous wings.

You can observe hundreds of monarch butterflies at Highway One near Pismo Beach, California. There are eucalyptus trees surrounding a park. You can hear about these butterflies several times a day. Butterflies mate in January.

Butterflies are delightful to observe. They move about in a creative manner. Their bright wings cheer us up. They add to nature's beauty.

# EIGHT

## *UMBRELLAS AND PARASOLS*

Umbrellas and parasols are useful and interesting to look at. Umbrellas are used during rainy days. Umbrellas shield people from pouring rain. They are handy to use to keep rain off of our clothes, hair and faces so we can protect our clothes and bodies.

Parasols are usually used by women during hot days in bright sunlight. Parasols are generally smaller and fancier than umbrellas. Parasols have lacy trimmings. Parasols are made with intricate designs. Women use parasols which match their lovely dresses. Parasols are feminine to look at.

Umbrellas have been used for hundreds of years to shield men, women and children from wet climate. As they step outside from their homes, cars, buses and trains many people depend on umbrellas.

Large umbrellas were used on chariots, wagons and buggies to protect passengers from rain and the hot, burning sun. Kings and queens as well as pharaohs and some Caesars were shielded with big umbrellas. They were fanned with large feathers to keep cooler. These feathers shielded leaders in hot climates during ancient times. Today, large umbrellas are often used on golf courses to shield players from the hot sun.

Umbrellas will continue to be made for rainy days and nights. They are useful and needed to shield people from wet weather. Parasols will stay in style for many years to come. They both are ingenious creations.

# NINE

## *STAINED GLASS OBJECTS*

Stained glass objects are unique and add colorful designs in churches, towers, temples and synagogues. Stained glass windows are picturesque with religious designs and icons. Designs of Jesus Christ and his disciples have been designed on stained glass windows. They stand out with distinction to impress passers-by.

Other stained glass objects are lamp shades, murals, wall settings and door windows. Jesus Christ churches have stained glass windows. Stained glass designs are colorful and unique. They add beautiful designs and colors in churches and public buildings.

Churches in Europe are known for many stained glass windows. They describe historical periods and important events in church history. Stained glass murals and windows are a fore of art depicting a way of life in earlier civilizations. Different religious scenes are vividly portrayed in churches.

Stained glass windows were created in the Middle Ages. Catholic priests, Catholic popes, prophets, archangels, other angels as well as shepherds and their sheep were designed in colored, stained glass.

Magnificent stained glass scenes were designed at Westminster Abbey in London, England, at Notre Dame Cathedral in Paris, France, and St. Mark's Cathedral in Venice, Italy. The larger the stained glass windows were, the larger the church was built. Stained glass windows are placed in front doors. They look spectacular and colorful. Homes with stained glass windows look more interesting. Stained glass windows add to a home's decor. They are added features.

Tiffany lamps are made with stained glass. There are standing lamps and table lamps. Each Tiffany lampshade is unique and carefully designed. There are flower designs and other nature designs plus geometric designs. Original Tiffany lamps made by Louis Comfort Tiffany are very valuable. Less expensive copies are available in most lamp stores.

Stained glass windows, murals, lamps and other objects are still popular. Stained glass is beautiful and picturesque. This is why stained glass is so popular and used.

# TEN

## *THE ETHERIC UNIVERSE*

The etheric universe is the invisible, permanent reality of universal creation. The etheric blueprint was crated before the physical manifestation took place.

Every thought, word and deed of every creature and think in the manifested universe is imprinted by Fohatic energy upon the great ocean of etheric substance which can be compared to a photographic image of the universe.

The study of geometry includes three powers, positive, negative and neutral, manifest in all things. The positive-negative, the Father or great creative power of the Universe gives power of thought, principle of Manas; the negative-positive pole manifests the thought by bringing it into form, or act.

"The neutral, or central point of the "line of life" attracts to itself both the power of projector and receiver." It fixes the image of the thought, word or deed, upon or within that Etheric Substance which in Geometry is illustrated by the square and in Arithmetic by the number 4. Here the image remains during the whole cycle of manifestation.

Astral light has two aspects or planes of consciousness. Its higher aspect is creative and preservative. From it are reflected or projected all inscribed principles of perfect form or order. The plane of soul manifestation is the reflected the same principles, plus what each soul many have gained by planetary life.

The lower aspect of the Astral Light is the plane of disorder and disintegration of form. From it we receive misqualified, unpleasant appearing forms. This is usually the first stopping place of a soul's experience after death before returning to Devachan, which is a higher state of etheric existence. The lower, astral plane is where we must become purged and purified from physical matter and dross.

"Spirit in bondage is spirit in torment." The lower, astral plane is an astral duplicate of the Earth. We see astral images of the Earth in the astral plane. Constituent elements are dissolved and transmuted.

Cause and effect are operating laws that help the universe to function in harmony and balance. The invisible planes such as the higher etheric, higher astral and lower astral planes affect each other. The etheric universe holds the physical universe together.

The law of centralization exists in the etheric universe. All life begins with a nucleus in the center. All lines of force come out from centers. Planets revolve around suns. Solar systems move around central suns. A blueprint exists in every star, sun, planet, planetoid. A divine plan of life exists from the largest to smallest living creation in the universe.

# ELEVEN

## *CHEMICAL AND ALCHEMICAL AFFINITY*

There is in face but one primal, all inclusive element and that is fire. Fire is creator and created, Cosmic Father, Mother, Brother and Sister with forty-nine aspects or principles. In manifestation as a single entity, it is first of all Intelligence.

We should focus on an action of subdivisions, energies and elements which are the secondary embodiment in intelligence. Oxygen is an element in Intelligence. It depends entirely upon the affinity for Oxygen existing in ay two or more elements whether it is possible for them to combine with each other and create or generate other elementary substances or energies.

The concealed fire, commonly termed heat, is the only form of energy which can break up the constituents of any elementary substance and compel them to combine with others in some other form of substance.

"With the first cyclic rise and fall of the Great Breath, the breathings, fiery forces, emanate and combine, thus creating the plane or state we call Intelligence. Each one of these breaths us a divine Spirit, an Entity, a God which yields up its manifested existence as one, to become many, a mode of motion which becomes many rates of vibration."

Every breath, every God or Monad is a distinct life, an identity which cannot be lost, whatever for or combination of forms the monadic essence (of which a Monad is an emanation) may create in Time and Space.

The before-mentioned breaths are four-fold or four-faced, so to speak. Each breath or degree of energy, contains all the potentialities of all positive and negative forces, yet it must combine with the succeeding breath – the next released energy or emanation – in order to create those four faces or aspects, and the two thus combined with their progeny – emanations – manifest the positive-negative and negative aspects of itself, the first square, which ultimately becomes the four planes of the Cosmos.

Chemical affinity occurs when oxygen and hydrogen is combined in balance to produce water. Water is valuable and needed on Earth. Purified water is healthy to use in daily life. Water is an important resource on Earth.

Oxygen is necessary to maintain life. Trees and other plants produce oxygen. Oxygen is a main source of necessary energy. Chemical affinity is produced in oxygen. The Great Breath is created from oxygen.

Oxygen and hydrogen are united to produce fire. Fire is an important element. Fire consumes other elements. Fire produces heat and energy necessary on Earth. Fire is useful and needed for many reasons.

Alchemical affinity can exist between souls. Each soul had an I Am Presence, the Father-God. Each soul has a Christ Self, the Mother-God. Each soul is a son or daughter of God on the physical plane. A trinity of Father-Mother-Son are alchemical components which work together for the spiritual evolution of the spirit of God. The positive relationship of matter, force and consciousness and spirit, consciousness and etheric awareness enhances souls to universal consciousness.

Every soul, known as a life spark, has the opportunity to live with love, unity, by the Golden Rule and in harmony with God and all life. We can become One with universal affinity.

# TWELVE

## *ABOUT LILIA FERNANDES,*
## *A TRUE STORY*

Lilia Fernandes grew up in Mexico in a small, Mexican village. Her parents were very strict and expected Lilia to behave with absolute respect and obedience. Lilia grew up with discipline and conservative values.

Lilia is one of four children. She remained petite with dark brown hair and brown eyes. She became a beautician when she was twenty years old. She dressed in dresses and attractive shoes. She curled her hair. She began wearing some facial makeup to appear more attractive.

Lilia is a very beautiful person. Yet she is not an immoral woman. She works hard as a beautician. When she was thirty she met her husband, Curtis Fernandes. He courted her for a period of time. After Lilia and Curtis were married Lilia became pregnant with her eldest child, Jefferey. He was born with a healthy body. Her second child, Sabrina, was born healthy. However, her third child, Revina, was born with severe handicaps. Lilia's blood type is RH. Her husband's blood type is not compatible with her RH blood type.

Revina was handicapped at birth. Lilia had to take care of Revina full time. Revina sleeps in the same bedroom with her mother. Lilia's husband sleeps in another bedroom because he doesn't want to wake up constantly to look after Revina.

Revina is attached to a machine which is used to suck out mucous from her throat. She is now four years old. Lilia gets up throughout the night to turn on the machine to clear Revina's mucous. She usually has had to get up six or more times in the night to care for her daughter. Revina does not have as many mucous attacks.

Lilia has hired a nurse to look after Revina from 10:00 a.m. until 6:00 p.m. five days a week. Lilia works five days a week as a beautician. She also cooks and cleans house when she is home.

Lilia continues to work hard as a beautician, a mother and she is a loyal wife and devoted mother. Revina goes to school. She joins several other children at public school. She sits in a wheelchair most of the time.

Lilia is a positive and pleasant person. She is unselfish and she is not spoiled. She is a reliable person. She is an excellent beautician and she owns her own beauty parlor. She is forty-four years old. She continues to work full time at her own beauty parlor.

# THIRTEEN

## *GOLDEN DAYS*

Golden days would exist for Christine and Douglas Wentworth who were now in their senior years. They had much more time to enjoy sunrises and sunsets. Christina and Douglas had worked hard since their teen days.

Now the Wentworths could relax and experience more time enjoying their retirement years. The days were gone when Christina and Douglas had to raise their three children. Their children were grown up and had left home to live independently.

Christina enjoyed cooking exotic food for Douglas. She sewed their clothes such as dresses, blouses, shirts, slacks, nightgowns and pajamas. Christina enjoyed caring for a garden in the front and back yards. She went outdoors regularly to water and weed her well-cultivated variety of plants and flowers.

Douglas liked to go fishing and hiking. He walked four miles almost every day. He was five feet ten inches in height.

He was able to play volleyball and tennis even though he was in his early seventies.

Christina and Douglas had time to go roaming on nearby beaches and to lagoons and scenic, national parks where there were evergreen trees and very fresh air to breathe freely.

Television programs such as soap operas, travelogues, special interest dramas, science, historical documentaries, gardening and a variety of music, TCM movies and other dramas were put on television for millions of people to watch. Christina and Douglas watched their favorite television programs. They also enjoyed reading.

The Wentworths went frequently to the public library. They examined many library books. They did research about many topics. They checked out a variety of books so they could enjoy reading. Christina enjoyed reading adventure and romance books. Douglas enjoyed travel and science fiction books. They both were avid readers.

Since Christina and Douglas were retired they had plenty of time to travel and to participate in different hobbies. Christina traveled vicariously by reading and imagining what it would be like to do the things mentioned in different books. She read several hours every day.

Douglas liked to explore interesting trails near the beaches. He walked for miles on dirt pathways. He saw sea birds, tree squirrels and different birds such as sparrows, sandpipers and seagulls. Douglas walked down to the beach and went swimming in the ocean.

Christina attended a Sewing Club where she participated in sewing clothes and quilts, etc. She was able to socialize with other women. She attended the Grange. She met new friends at the Grange. She learned about the regional environment and farming techniques to help a farm thrive.

Christina and Douglas went dancing at a barn in the village they lived in. They square danced in groups of four couples. Guitars were played. Country music was heard which couples danced to. Christina and Douglas participated in a variety of square dancing patterns. They strengthened their legs and arms. The exercise was healthy.

At the square dance Christina and Douglas met other couples. They made more new friends. Christine and Douglas were enjoying these golden days of their retirement years.

# FOURTEEN

## *AVATARS EXIST*

An Avatar is a divine incarnation known as an exalted being. An Avatar is a world teacher. Who are Avatars? Jesus Christ was an Avatar or world teacher.

"There are many degrees of Avatars. There are many Christs. The one known as Jesus incarnated in 2,000 year cycles for long ages, teaching the evolution of our humanity," Harold Forgostein stated, who was the fourth Guardian-in-Chief of the Temple of the People in Halcyon, California.

We are taught that Buddha, Krishna, Osaris, Hermes and Hiawatha and more are all Avatars who serve humanity. The Temple of the People believes in the nativity story about Jesus Christ. The Temple teaches that an Avatar comes to His people when the need is greatest, when the times are bleakest, devoid of life and growth, the spirit subdued, subject to harshest conditions.

The idea of hope for mankind is embodied in the New Testament story which only echoes countless others. The saving grace of humanity is born in the most humble of surroundings and recognized by the wise of each age, whether poor or wealthy.

"The Temple was formed to continue the work of providing a nucleus for the formation of the brother/sisterhood of humanity," Harold Forgostein stated. Temple members were told in the beginning days that their mission was, as John the Baptist, to announce the coming of the Avatar for this cycle and prepare a place for Him to work from and with, just as John had done 2,000 years ago for Jesus.

"The Temple teaches that the Great Soul began to establish renewed evidence of an Avatar's power around the beginning of this century and that influence had reached to its full maturity about thirty years later," Harold Forgostein said.

The Temple teaches that great cycles of time govern the action of the lesser ones, just as the larger gear wheels in a clockworks control the smaller ones. One of the cycles was short allowing for the birth and growth to maturity of the new Avatar on Inner planes. The Avatar's degree of evolutionary power gave Him that capacity.

How can we recognize an Avatar? We can recognize an Avatar through his or her light and higher vibration. An Avatar maintains higher consciousness with God's wisdom and truth. An Avatar teaches others to seek peace, light and truth. An Avatar helps to change the world and to make the world a better place to live.

# FIFTEEN

## *SANTA CLAUS*

The spirit of Christmas is increased because of the jolly, generous spirit known to be Santa Claus. Santa Claus is known to be Saint Nicholas. There was a real Nicholas Kringle who traveled around to give gifts to many people. Saint Nicholas was a jolly, generous person. He drove around in a sleigh to deliver gifts to villagers.

Christmas is a time to be joyful and appreciative about the birth of Jesus Christ. Christmas means Christ Mass. Christians have participated in church Mass to pray and sing about Jesus Christ's birth and role as the Messiah.

Santa Claus is a symbol of giving. Santa Claus comes on his sleigh over the sky to everyone's home to deliver gifts. He goes down chimneys after people are in bed. He leaves gifts for many children. They must be well behaved to receive gifts. Otherwise Santa Claus will not distribute gifts to naughty children.

Christmas is celebrated every year. It is a time to display

Christmas decorations, sing songs such as Christmas carols, to have parties and to appreciate the birth of Jesus Christ.

Santa Claus may be accepted for many generations to come. It is traditional to decorate one's home with a Christmas tree, Christmas stockings and to open Christmas gifts on Christmas day. Christmas cookies, pies and eggnog are enjoyed.

Christmas is a holiday which may be celebrated every year for many years to come. Christianity is a popular religion in Europe and the Americas. Many people believe in the teachings of Jesus Christ, who is the Messiah and prophet 2,000 years ago.

# SIXTEEN

## *PROCELAIN PARAPHERNALIA*

Many porcelain items are created for displays and decorations. Porcelain is usually white and blue. Blue designs and nature scenes are painted onto bowls, jars, dishes, cups and figurines.

Chinese people are well known for creating porcelain objects. Many art museums display ancient, porcelain items. Large, Chinese vases are colorful with porcelain covered designs. Chinese porcelain vases and jars are priceless today. The war worth a great deal because they are ancient and no longer designed today.

Europeans in Holland, Germany, Switzerland and Great Britain, etc, porcelain plates, vases, cups, pitchers, ladles, bowls and other objects have been created for art display. These porcelain artifacts are displayed on tables and shelves in restaurants and homes. Europeans are artistic and creative. Many pottery makers and porcelain designers are able to create many artistic designs.

Artistic creations are beautiful to look at in restaurants,

museums and homes. They add real personality and a creative touch. Porcelain objects are not made so much today. Many artistic creations are made with glass, plastic and wood. Some artistic objects are made with brass and metal.

Porcelain art is still impressive. Many porcelain objects are sold in tourist places like Solvang, California. Import shops usually have porcelain artifacts. Import shops exist in large cities throughout the world.

So, decorate your home with porcelain dishes, bowls, plates, ladles and figurines. These artifacts will add a special flair to your home.

# SEVENTEEN

## *FRAME YOUR PHOTOS AND PAINTINGS*

Pictures and paintings look much better when they are placed in frames. Frames also protect photos, pictures and paintings. Frame shops offer a variety of frames. There are wood, metal and metallic frames.

Frames must fit photos, pictures and paintings. The size of each frame must be the exact size to place photos, pictures and paintings in. Some frames have glass covers that seal pictures, photos and paintings from direct contact with air.

Some frames have designs on the rimmings or sidings. Other frames are stained in different colors such as red, blue, brown, yellow and tan. The upper and lower corners are fitted together and screwed in or nailed together. Frames may be wedged together in the upper right and left corners and lower right and left corners.

Photos, pictures and paintings last much longer and do not fade when they are put into frames. Frames are useful and valuable. They help make photos, pictures and paintings look much more attractive and professional looking.

Some frames are inexpensive while other frames are expensive. Some frames may look expensive. Yet these frames are reasonably priced.

Photo frames are usually very reasonable at Wal Mart, K Mart, Rite Aid and other discount stores. Many family photos can be put in one large frame. Some photo frames are gold or silver with narrow rims around the photos and pictures.

Frame shops exist in towns and cities across our nation and other countries. There are a variety of shops and frame makers that provide a variety of frames. They are willing to put paintings, photos and pictures in frames for their customers.

# EIGHTEEN

## *CREEKSIDE ADVENTURES*

Creeks exist in many locations in the world. Adventures can occur in and along creeks. Tim Sheldon and Ed Landis were close friends from early childhood. They often went on adventures into forests and mountains.

Now Tim and Ed decided to walk along a long creek near their village. They wore rubber boots and climbing outfits. They went close to the embankment of the wide, cool creek. The creek water was flowing to the south. Many rocks and stones were in the creek.

Frogs were croaking in the grass near the creek. Some frogs leaped into the creek and swam to rocks in the creek. The creek was approximately four feet deep in the center. Tim and Ed looked into the creek and they saw minnows, yellow fin fish, trout and many polliwogs.

Ed and Tim tried to capture some frogs. They leaped away before either Ed or Tim could catch them. Ed and Tim decided to walk into the creek and walk downstream. They wore their boots to protect their feet from rocks and hard stones. They continued walking in the creek. Fresh water fish swam past them in a southern direction. The creek water splashed against Ed and Tim's legs up to their upper backs. The water was cold. They shivered in the creek.

Ed and Tim waded through the creek for some time. They became tired. So they walked out of the creek. They sat on an embankment to rest and to dry off. The sun blazed down onto them. Their clothes began to dry off.

Tim said, "Let's find out where this creek leads after we have rested for a while." Ed replied, "Good idea. We need to continue walking West." After Tim and Ed rested for a while they continued walking West along the creek embankment. They walked for a least an hour until they came to the ocean.

The creek water flowed into the ocean into two streams of water directly into the ocean. Ed and Tim were fascinated the way the creek water flowed into the ocean. They observed the seagulls and sandpipers flocking around on the beach and in the sky near the ocean.

Tim and Ed walked back along the creekside in a northern direction. They went back to the location they had started from. They reached their destination late in the afternoon. The sun was beginning to set.

Along the way back Tim and Ed wore their rubber boots. They saw more frogs and fish in the creek water. The creek sparkled as water flowed swiftly toward the south. Tim and Ed's northward trek back to their village was adventurous. There were squirrels scurrying on the ground in nearby woodlands near the creek. Some squirrels climbed up and down tree trunks and branches. They had long, bushy tails.

Some squirrels were gathering pine nuts to take to their nests. Some squirrels were standing near the edge of the creek sipping creek water. They rushed away when they saw Tim and Ed walking toward them along the side of the creek. Blue jays, red breasted robins and sparrows were flying around and chirping in the nearby woods.

Tim and Ed were almost back to where they started their journey. They had observed what was happening around them. Beautiful crimson, orange and reddish-yellow colors began to reflect through the trees in rays of light because the sun was setting. Tim and Ed saw a mother deer and her baby fawn lying down under some trees. This was a picturesque scene.

Finally Tim and Ed returned to their homes in their village in Newberry, Kentucky. They had enjoyed their creekside adventures.

# NINETEEN

## *JAPANESE BATHS*

Japanese people are know for their Japanese baths. They build deep, wooden pools. They fill hot water in the deep pool. When the water is steaming hot, Japanese men and women bathe publicly in the nude. Japanese men usually bathe on one side of the pool. Japanese women bathe on the other side of the pool. They are courteous in the pool. Japanese men do not pursue Japanese women in the pool.

It is a custom to bathe at least once a day in the bathing room. Japanese men and women use towels to dry off. They go back to where their clothes are available. They finish drying off and then they get dressed.

The Japanese pools and tubs are drained, re-cleaned and filled with clean water, which is heated for the next bath. Bathing is a special and sacred occasion. Japanese people stay clean because they bathe regularly.

# TWENTY

## *RUSSIAN VILLAGE LIFE*

Many Russians live in villages in different provinces in the Soviet Union. Russian villages usually have wooden homes with space for animals such as cows, goats and domestic pets. Dogs and cats live in villages.

Russian families live in villages. Generally they exchange food and goods. Some families produce milk and cheese. Other families may produce fresh vegetables. Other families may product fresh fruit. Leather goods are exchanged.

Russian people receive groceries at grocery exchange places in villages and cities. Russian people are assigned to different jobs and occupations by the Communist government.

Soviet Union people also live in Democratic states such as Georgia. They attend village meetings to share community events. A villager may attend a town hall to watch television. They all watch programs on one television in the community.

Russians have maintained their traditions and certain customs. They like to perform in Russian folk dances. They play guitars and sing well known Russian folk songs. Many folk dances and folk songs describe the way of life and beliefs of early Russians. Russian costumes are worn. Traditional dances are performed by Russian people.

Different seasonal events take place in Russian villages. Artistic, Russian dolls are created and are appreciated by many Russians. The wooden dolls are very colorful and depict the way traditional costumes are painted on the wooden dolls.

Russians have learned to produce zithers, banjos and quality guitars. Many Russian folk singers play their string instruments while they sing historical folk songs.

Russians have learned to adapt to Communism. Some Soviet Union people have learned to live in government housing. They are paid government salaries to use to pay for groceries, clothes, household items and transportation. They accept the salaries the government pays them.

Russians have gone back to worship God and Jesus Christ. Russians celebrate harvest time. They prepare delicious, Russian foods to share in the villages. Harvest time is a very important time during different seasons. Fresh crops, wheat, oats, vegetables and fruits are harvested.

Farmers' Markets exist in the Soviet Union. Fresh vegetables and fruits are selected at the Farmers' Markets. This is a good way to select the best, fresh resources when they become available.

Russian villagers are family minded. They become closer together because of their village life. Their music, dancing, traditional beliefs and religious beliefs bring them closer together. They help one another during crises as well as joyful times. Many Russian people want to live in peace and harmony.

# TWENTY-ONE

## *EDGAR CAYCE INSIGHTS*

Edgar Cayce was a psychic during the twentieth century. He was a sleeping prophet. He was able to reveal past catastrophes, cataclysms and earthquakes. He was able to reveal future predictions such as World Wars I, II and other wars.

Edgar Cayce wrote <u>There Is A River</u> which describes the reality of reincarnation. He was able to reveal thousands of incarnations and embodiments of his clients. Memories have been recalled from past lives.

Edgar Cayce spoke about life of ancient Lemurians, Atlanteans, Egyptians and other civilizations. He predicted that modern civilizations would repeat habits that would lead them eventually into diseases and that modern civilizations will begin to perish.

Edgar Cayce wrote <u>Lemuria And Atlantis</u> and <u>Akashic Records</u>. He spoke about how both Lemuria and Atlantis fell into the ocean because of cataclysms and severe earthquakes which suddenly appeared. He predicted enormous tidal waves that would change conditions on the Earth's surface.

Edgar Cayce became aware of reincarnation because the embodiments of hundreds of people were revealed to him. He realized that we are born again and again even though we maintain the same soul. Reincarnation is part of God's cycle. Humanity has the opportunity to grow and serve the Earth. Many incarnations are necessary to learn and to evolve on Earth.

Edgar Cayce was given information about clients' lives. He learned about different civilizations and customs of different civilizations. He found out about Lemuria and Atlantis when he heard about different embodiments from different individuals who revealed details about their lives. He recorded their past life experiences in <u>There Was A River</u> and <u>Akashic Records</u> and <u>Lemuria And Atlantis</u>.

Edgar Cayce diagnosed many diseases. He told people how to become cured from these diseases with natural herbs and natural cures. Doctors eventually agreed with Edgar Cayce's natural cures.

Edgar Cayce's prophesies from the 1920s to 1980s have come true. He predicted World War One and Two. He also predicted the Great Depression. He predicted the John F. Kennedy assassination. He predicted the 2012 A.D catastrophes, cataclysms and sudden changes.

Edgar Cayce mentioned warnings about future dangers and destruction. He told people to overcome destructive habits. He stated that humanity would eventually perish if changes for peace and goodwill don't take place.

# TWENTY-TWO

## *AVOIDING ACCIDENTS*

We usually get in an accident when we least expect it. Even if you are a good driver you may encounter a sudden situation where you may lose control. Then you are in an accident.

Mary Ann Foster was an excellent driver. She had been driving for many years. One day she drove to a scenic area near a lagoon. As she approached the lagoon a dog ran from the right side of her car directly into the front of her car. Mary Ann quickly swirled her car to the left side of the road.

Mary Ann's car ran into a steel rail on the left side of a narrow bridge. Her car crashed suddenly so that it was badly damaged. Meanwhile, the dog had run off unharmed.

Mary Ann received a cut lip, scratches on both of her knees and bruises in her mid rib area. She managed to endure this accident while the dog ran off unharmed! Mary Ann was glad she didn't kill the dog. However, she suffered because she tried to avoid hitting the dog with her car.

If Mary Ann stayed on the street without swerving away from the dog which ran in front of her car she most likely would have hit and killed the stray dog. She may have avoided damaging her car. Was this the best choice to make? Mary Ann didn't think so because she didn't want to kill the dog.

Bill Morgan drove a truck for a living. He brought strong, hot coffee with him on his truck route in order to keep awake. He had been driving a truck for fourteen years and he was a careful driver.

As Bill was driving a company truck one night he was on the freeway heading south toward Los Angeles, California. It was about 10:45 p.m. on December 21, 2005. Bill was driving in the right hand lane at about 52 miles an hour. Suddenly a four-door sedan Buick drove swiftly in the left lane near him. The driver was speeding on the freeway.

The driver in the Buick impatiently moved about in different lanes to get around different cars. Suddenly the traffic was stacked up on the freeway. Bill Morgan stayed in the far right lane. The driver in the Buick decided to get in the far right lane. Evidently the driver headed into the far right lane to exit from the freeway.

The driver, known as Stanley Tollen, a teenager, quickly moved in front of Bill Morgan's truck without a right hand signal on. His Buick was too close to the truck. Bill slammed on his brakes to avoid hitting Stanley Tollen's Buick. However, it was difficult to slow his truck down in time.

Bill Morgan accidentally hit and rammed into Stanley Tollen's car. Stanley's car rammed into the car in front of him. Stanley's car went out of control. Several other nearby cars hit Stanley's car because his car swerved into several cars. Stanley's car was badly damaged. He was wounded during his accident.

At least a dozen cars as well as Bill Morgan's truck were stacked up on the freeway. Bill's truck was slightly nicked. The other cars were damaged more. A woman had a cell phone. She called the nearest police station to report the accident.

Bill Morgan was not physically injured in his big truck. His front bumper had a few scratches. Stanley's car was demolished. He was badly injured. He received a concussion in his head and he broke several ribs. He had lacerations on his arms and legs. He barely escaped being killed.

People in several other cars were injured and their cars were damaged. An ambulance and several police cars arrived at the accident within fifteen minutes. Stanley Tollen and several other people were taken to the nearest Emergency Ward in the nearby area.

This car accident could have been avoided if Stanley Morgan had not moved quickly without warning to the far right lane. It was dark out which may have added to the accident. Stanley was careless and he did not use his blinker. He should have waited before driving into the far right lane. If he hadn't been so careless other drivers and passengers would not have been in an accident. Stanley would need to be much more careful if he drove in the future.

# TWENTY-THREE

## *INTO THE LIGHT*

Light exists in the Cosmos. Light is the source of God energy which emanates throughout the Cosmic Plan. Within the light God energy emerges in all life.

Within the light the flow of God's love, purity, unity, harmony and balance manifests. Light is the giver of fohatic energy which functions in every cell in the nucleus, atoms and electrons.

Light is the source of being. Light heals us with its purifying rays. Light restores us constantly. The light of God never fails. We need to call the light of God into action.

Let us walk in the light. Let us love the light. Let us be one with the light. Let us be healed by God's light. Let us recognize the light. Let us appreciate the light within us.

Light dissolves darkness. Light restores life. Light is the source of our being on seven planes. Let us live in the light.

# TWENTY-FOUR

## *EFFECTS OF PAINKILLERS*

Painkillers are often used to help stop pain in our bodies. Generally Bayer Aspirin, Tylenol Extra Strength, Tylenol #3 with Codeine and Vicodin are prescribed to lessen body pains and muscular pains and spasms.

Generally two tablets are taken every five or six hours over a period of several days. It is wise to go to see your family doctor to be sure he or she can diagnose the problem and possible causes regarding the pains.

Tylenol Extra Strength is usually 500 mg per tablet. So if two tablets are taken a person has 1,000 mg of Tylenol. Some pain may be eliminated. If the symptoms continue this is a sign that indicates that Tylenol has not cured the problem.

Tylenol #3 with Codeine may constipate a person. It takes time to heal the constipation. The best remedy for constipation is to stop taking Tylenol #3. Use Miralax laxative powder once or twice a day to help you overcome constipation from using Tylenol #3 with Codeine.

Some doctors prescribe Vicodin to decrease physical pain.

However, Vicodin has more side effects. A person can become dizzy. He or she may experience stomach aches. A person should not drive if he or she has taken Vicodin because the driver may become drowsy.

Morphine is a strong painkiller. Yet the side effects from morphine are not pleasant. Numbness, drowsiness and constipation can occur. Morphine should be taken in small doses. It is dangerous to become addicted to morphine. Too much morphine can cause serious consequences such as severe constipation and cramps.

Pain killers may help alleviate some pain. Don't depend on painkillers over a long period of time. You may become addicted. Side effects can cause more physical problems. So, be careful what painkillers to take. Be sure to avoid becoming addicted to any painkillers.

# TWENTY-FIVE

## *ECHOES FROM THE PAST*

Echoes of the past remind us of past experiences. Fond memories of yesteryear help us realize why life is so worthwhile day by day and year by year. We appreciate our happy memories. We rejoice at the wonderful times and highlights that have occurred in our lives.

Betsy Harris recalled pleasant memories of her childhood years in Penten Beach, California. She had made many childhood friends and acquaintances. Betsy was well liked in school and in her neighborhood.

Betsy reminisced about her life. She thought about the time she went to camp at an all girls' camp at Big Bear Lake in San Bernardino, California. Betsy went on trail hikes to observe plants and animals. She learned about wild flowers, fauna, lichen, mosses and ferns. She gathered plant specimens to study them.

Big Bear Lake was an enormous lake. Residents and tourists go boating, fishing and swimming in this lake. Betsy went swimming in Big Bear Lake. She enjoyed boating there as well. She went boating with camper friends.

Betsy spent three months at camp near Big Bear Lake. She made friends with many of the girls who attended camp. She recalled her visits with them. She became fond of her new friends.

Betsy went home from the girls' camp at the end of summer vacation. She managed to take a variety of photographs of her new friends and of her camping experiences. Her photographs turned out very good. She placed many of her photographs into photo albums.

Betsy showed her photo albums to her neighborhood friends and relatives. She valued her photographs. She spoke to her friends and relatives about her experiences as she showed her photographs.

Jimmy Nelsen recalled his experiences in high school and college. He was a good student in high school and college. Jimmy was in his forties now. He worked in a bank as an administrator. His job at the bank was not really that stimulating or interesting.

Jimmy tended to recall his past memories because his present life was not interesting. He recalled playing football in high school. He played well and he became a high school football hero. He was given a lot of recognition as a top football player.

Jimmy played tennis, volleyball, kickball, basketball and hockey in high school. He was a top player in each of these sports. He enjoyed being an active, outdoor person. He still played tennis and volleyball with friends. He continued to participate in outdoor sports.

Echoes from our past alert us because our memories are part of our conscious awareness. Out past is part of our present and future because we focus on flashbacks regularly that cause us to respond to our memories of the past.

# TWENTY-SIX

## *USE OF VCRS AND DVD PLAYERS*

Today VCRs, known to be video cassette players, are commonly played at home. A variety of videos can be played in a VCR. Videos can be checked out from a public library. You can select Hollywood films, travelogues, religious films, documentaries which are historical and scientific.

People who view videos have the opportunity to see movies from the 1920s through 2008. That's Entertainment I, II, III and IV are very popular videos. Entertainment performed with solos, dancers and actors. Broadway excerpts have been presented in That's Entertainment.

DVD players receive discs. Each disc is made from a recording made into sound track and visual production from a recorded disc. These discs are lightweight and easy to carry around. Each disc is played in a DVD player. DVD players can be carried wherever a person goes. They can be used in cars and taken just about anywhere such as restaurants and people's homes because they are portable.

# TWENTY-SEVEN

## *LIGHTHOUSES BEACON*

Lighthouses exist in major harbors. A lighthouse is a tall, cylindrical building on a large rock foundation near manmade peninsulas. A lighthouse beams light to warn people in boats, cargo ships and cruisers that they are close to shore. God and heavy clouds can block off boats from the coastline.

Lighthouses have been built all over the world. They are significant landmarks in the ocean or in the harbor. Their flashing lights are so bright that their flashing beams can be seen many miles away. Their beacon lights make a difference because their flashing lights blaze across the sky lighting up the ocean and the harbor.

San Luis Obispo Lighthouse is located in Avila Bay Harbor in California. A beacon light flashes every night from a peninsula where the lighthouse stands. All the fishermen are alerted by the flashing light from the San Luis Obispo Lighthouse.

Lighthouse attendants walk up stairways to an upper room where large, beacon lights are stored. The attendants check the beacon lights to be sure they will turn on when it starts to get dark. They replace lights that have burned out.

Lighthouse attendants guard lighthouses. They make sure no one vandalizes the lighthouse. Lighthouses are valuable because their beacon lights are warnings to passers-by in vessels, boats and cruisers that land is nearby.

The world's first lighthouse was the Pharos of Alexandria. The immense tower lit the harbor for more than a thousand years. This first century lighthouse, now in ruins, helped Roman ships navigate around the tiny island of Capri just south of Naples.

The rays of the setting sun peek through the lens of the inactive Cape Meares Lighthouse making it appear to be lit. Nicknamed "Old Baldy," the Bald Head Lighthouse is the oldest of North Carolina's many lighthouses. The 1818 tower, originally known as Cape Fear Lighthouse, was deactivated in 1935 and is now open to the public as a museum.

The Skerriyvate Lighthouse off the coast of Scotland was built to withstand the punishing currents of the North Sea. The wild seas and jagged rocks seen in Thomas Cole's View across Frenchman's Bay from Mount Desert Island after a squall. 1845 clearly illustrates why a long-time commissioner of the Bureau of Lighthouses considered the station at Mount Desert Rock to be the most exposed in the whole United States.

Dangerous, rocky shores require reliable lights for the most practical of reasons, but the nature of these rugged settings make lighthouses picturesque photography subjects. Now inactive, Price Creek Lighthouse was erected to guide vessels through the mouth of the Cape Fear River, part of a dangerous expanse of waters along the southern coast of North Carolina.

Now restored to its original appearance, Split Rock Lighthouse possesses one of the country's most spectacular lighthouse settings. The promontory soars 130 feet over Lake Superior. When Florida joined the United States in 1821, St. Augustine Lighthouse was finally built to provide enough light over the harbor in 1874 at Anastasia Island, Florida.

Cape Lookout Lighthouse, built in 1859, has a unique diamond, daymark pattern. Daymarks are used to make lighthouses more visible when the sun is shining in northern climates. They also help make these landmarks stand out in the snow.

Eldred Rock Lighthouse, one of the state's oldest surviving lights, was constructed in 1906 to guide vessels along the Lynn Canal in Haines, Alaska. The distinctive daymark pattern of West Quoddy Head Lighthouse has made it one of the country's best known lighthouses. Situated at the easternmost point of the continental United States, this famous light helps steer vessels through the Bay of Fundy in Lubec, Maine.

The sturdy masonry complex of Admiralty Head Lighthouse, built in 1903, contained a fourth order Fresnel lens that served until 1927. After years of disuse, this structure is now refurbished and is open to the public at Coupesville, Washington.

Many lighthouses have been built and maintained as landmarks and preserved as historical domains.

# TWENTY-EIGHT

## *OLD VICTORIAN HOUSES*

Old Victorian houses have been built throughout America. In San Luis Obispo County, California there are some Victorian homes. The Old Sands Victorian home in Oceano, California is near Highway One.

The Old Sands Victorian home is three stories. A gable roof exists at the top of this structure. There are unique window sidings in the top story near the gable section. The Victorian house is white and gray. The pointed, gable roof stands out. The rippled shingles are unique and can be seen from the road.

Victorian houses were created in Great Britain during Queen Victoria's reign. She was queen of Great Britain for approximately sixty years. She had architects design gable homes in Great Britain. Victorian homes became popular especially in the cities of London, Leister, Manchester, Liverpool, Norwich and South Hampton.

In San Luis Obispo, California there are a variety of

Victorian houses in a certain area where older, nineteenth century houses were built.

Victorian homes were built in San Francisco, California in the 1850s, one next to another. At least 50,000 Victorian homes were built before 1906. During a severe earthquake in 1906 thousands of homes were destroyed. Only 13,437 Victorian homes survived in San Francisco in 1906.

Author Allison Kyle Leopold feels that Victorian decorations and adornments were undertaken with a determination that bordered on evangelistic fervor. Artists and craftsmen used wood, metal, glass, upholstery, curtains, paint and paper and worked hard to fulfill the new desire for domestic comfort and romantic shadows.

Victorian homes have marked similarities. Notice high ceilings, gleaming wood floors, vintage mantels decorated with tile work, pocket doors dividing front and back parlors, painted or stained woodwork, ornate furniture, and eclectic collections of art and figurines in all periods and styles from ancient Egyptian to Art Nouveau.

Victorian houses have parlors or drawing rooms which are more beautiful and elegant than any other rooms in the house. The most cherished pieces of art and furniture were placed there. Mirrors brighten the dining room. Lace curtains existed. Colorful carpets lined the rooms. Long, wood staircases existed to get to upper floors.

Most Victorian houses were built in one of the three, basic, San Francisco styles: Italianate, Stick or Stick/Eastlake and Queen Ann. The Victorian queen of Pacific Heights is the Haas-Lilienthal House at 2007 Franklin, one of the finest Victorian houses in San Francisco.

Pacific Heights Library adopted the Victorian tradition of creating a Turkish or Moorish hideaway. Seven colors were used to add color to this Victorian house. The Pacific Heights gracious, dining room overlooks San Francisco Bay. The elaborately carved, built-in, china closet, with thistly, Louis Sullivanesque carvings, showcases the dinnerware.

Between Laguna and Octavia a row of Italianate, Victorian houses with octagonal bays and Stick entrances were built in the early 1870s by Thomas Martin. The new color designs harmonize well with each other and the neighborhood. At Pine between Laguna and Buchanan in 1889, San Francisco this Stick house was built by William Hinkel as part of a row of three houses. These classic houses were dressed in yellow and white with ochre and blue highlights. New owners have transformed it with eighties shades of teal, blues and grays.

An 1890 Victorian house between Buchanan and Webster near Pine in San Francisco has stained glass windows. This house is pale red, brandywine, three taupes, dark blue-gray and gold leaf. The unusual swirled columns are artfully picked out in gold and burgundy. In 1978 the doors were the most colorful portals. At an 1881 Victorian house between Webster and Fillmore, Italianate designer Butch Kardum chose two blues, apricot, creamy white and burgundy-brown to illuminate the pierced, wood balustrade, incised panels, paneled frieze and the unusual angled doorway of these row houses.

Situated between Steiner and Pierce there is an 1884 Stick/Queen Anne Victorian house. Robert Dufort of Magic Brush provided restoration and the burgundy, blues, grays and cream color scheme for the "if-we've-got-it-let's-use-it architecture." The rare colonettes architectural friezes and turret with soaring gables are highlighted with controlled color.

On Sacramento between Steiner and Pierce an 1884

Queen Anne Victorian row house is owned for thirty-eight years by a lady. In 1986 she decided to change the exterior of her house. She had cheerful colors painted such as blue, white and yellow designs. Her Victorian house looks bright and cheerful at the present time.

Victorian homes are three and four stories high with gabled roofs, shutters and fancy paneling and trims. The houses are built with up staircases. There are fireplaces in the parlor, bedrooms, living room and dining room. Chandeliers hang from the living rooms and dining rooms in most Victorian homes.

The Westerfeld Mansion, the Archbishop's Mansion and 1347 McAllister are three of the most architecturally significant buildings in the city of San Francisco. The Chateau Tivoli at 1057 Steiner at the corner of Golden Gate, a bed-and-breakfast scheduled to open in 1990, is also one of the finest Victorian houses in the city as well as being the greatest "Painted Lady" in the world.

Doug Butler's home at 1679 McAllister is the most colorful Victorian house in town. The Alamo Square area presents visitors with a staggering amount of extraordinary architecture and color design, and the collection continues to grow. A number of these Victorian homes are open either on a tour or because they are "B&Bs" or available to rent for special events.

# TWENTY-NINE

## *EXPERIENCING DIABETES*

Diabetes is a well known disease. People with Diabetes have pancreas dysfunctions. There are two types of Diabetes. People with Diabetes One can control their blood sugar by carefully eating food low in sugar and carbohydrates. They should avoid rich desserts and high cholesterol foods.

People with Diabetes Two must take insulin to control their blood sugar. If a person's blood sugar rises above 150 it is necessary to take some type of insulin to bring the blood sugar down to normal. Blood sugar should be between 90 to 110.

Diabetes can be controlled by careful eating habits and exercise. A nutritious breakfast is the way to begin each day. Boiled or sautéed eggs mixed with herbs is delicious. Sliced fruit such as a pear, an apple or strawberries add to breakfast. A bowl of cereal with low fat soya milk and sugar substitute adds fiber and vitamins to this morning meal. Insulin should be taken at least fifteen minutes before each meal. The insulin controls the blood sugar in a person's pancreas.

A Diabetes Two person should be very careful what he or she eats so the insulin will work to control blood sugar. Lean meats, raw vegetables and raw fruit and steamed vegetables, brown rice and some potatoes and powdered, soya blend are put in breakfast cereals without sugar. Use Stevia sugar substitute in your cereal.

Avoid eating cake, pies, cookies, rich puddings, ice cream and candy. High sugar desserts and snacks are not good to eat. Don't purchase them at the store to tempt you to eat improperly. Think about staying healthy.

How can a person know if he or she has Diabetes? A person can ask to have a blood test taken for blood sugar. If the blood test indicates there is more than the regular, normal sugar in the blood a person will be told by the blood lab results by the lab department at any hospital. One's family doctor can prescribe for a blood test. The doctor sends the patient's blood in a tube to the lab to determine blood sugar results.

Signs of Diabetes are dizzy spells, flashing white light in one's eyes, grogginess and shakiness from hypoglycemia. A person who does not control his or her blood sugar may feel very tired and worn out. Blurry eyes are another symptom.

It is wise to have an annual checkup every year. Blood tests should be taken at least two or three times a year. A person with Diabetes may acquire edema in his or her legs. Blurry, poor vision can occur because of high blood sugar. Body weaknesses may be other symptoms of Diabetes.

Diabetes can cause a person to have kidney failure, edema and possible cancers. So, take care of yourself. Eat carefully and have plenty of sleep and rest in order to maintain better health.

# THIRTY

## *SEASHORE PAINTINGS*

The views at various seashores are breathtaking. An artist can sketch the general landscape against the sea view. Seascapes are picturesque and scenic.

Artists use vivid colors to illustrate sunsets over a tranquil sea. Orange, purple, crimson and red add to the sunsets. Different cloud patterns make sunsets interesting to watch. The sun continues to move slowly over the horizon to create brilliant light.

Blue, purple and green as well as touches of orangish-red hues reflect over the ocean. Artists are capable of creating very vivid ocean colors over rippling currents and waves.

Beaches usually exist near the shore at oceans and sea sides. The drifting sand changes with contrasting colors. Some artists paint the seashore in the foreground.

A seashore painting when completed can be a wonderful ocean view to behold. Many people like to display seascapes in their living room and lounge.

David Mallory produced oil paintings of sea views in

Shell Beach and Pismo Beach, California. He is an excellent artist. He began painting while he was attending high school. He continued to paint throughout his life. His paintings are displayed in different art galleries in California. He paints with an original style. He has painted many seascapes. Many of his recent paintings are displayed in his own art gallery in Chico, California.

Artists have learned how to apply their paintbrushes to brush colors onto canvases. They blend lighter colors over darker colors in water color scenes. Then artists blend darker colors over lighter oil colors in oil paintings.

Seashore paintings are popular. People who appreciate paintings often select seascapes at art galleries to display in their homes. Seashore paintings add to the exotic, scenic beauty of people's homes.

# THIRTY-ONE

## *GAMES AND PUZZLES*

Games and puzzles are entertaining and fun to participate in. Both children and adults share games and puzzles at home and at friends' homes. Scrabble, Monopoly, checkers, chess, cards and other games are played.

Outdoor games are baseball, basketball, tetherball, hockey, hopscotch, volleyball, tennis, miniature golf and more. Other indoor games are ping pong, bowling and pool.

Puzzles are fascinating to put together. Each piece of a puzzle must fit in the correct place in order to complete a puzzle. There are many kinds of puzzles. Maps can be made into puzzles. There are animal, number and geometric design puzzles.

Games and puzzles are worthwhile activities for different age groups to participate in. When it is raining and too cold to play outdoors family members and friends are able to play indoor games. They are able to spend leisure time sharing indoor activities and games.

It is important to follow directions and the play fair while playing games. Being a good sport is important in order to maintain harmony and pleasant feelings. The purpose of playing games is to have fun and to participate in enjoyable activities to preoccupy their time.

Puzzles can be educational because a person can learn about geography, geometry, designs and people, etc. Fitting puzzle pieces together takes alertness and perception.

Indoor games and puzzles make wonderful gifts at Christmas, birthdays and other occasions. Games are worth receiving and playing. It is fun to share games and puzzles.

# THIRTY-TWO

## *UP IN THE ATTIC*

Many homes have attics above the ceiling or upstairs at the top of the house. Attics are usually places to store household things and memorable items in treasure boxes and chests.

Attics are generally dark and some of them are covered with webs and even dust because attics are often left unattended. Old furniture, chinaware, glass objects, old lamps, stored paintings, clothes worn by grandparents and other ancestors.

Attics can be used to store valuable family treasures and memorable items. Wedding dresses and prom dresses are often stored in clothing chests. Photographs are kept in photo albums.

At times family members may go into the attic to search for interesting things hidden in boxes and chests. Old wooden dolls may be stored in chests. Other wooden, carved objects such as horses, bears and rabbits. Old Hitty porcelain dolls are hundreds of years old. They may be stored in attics.

Patty and Selma Johnson lived in an old Victorian home

in San Francisco, California. They liked to play in their bedrooms. One day they decided to explore upstairs in the attic. They went upstairs to the third floor up narrow stairs.

There were dozens of boxes of things stored in the attic over many years. The attic was on the third floor. Curtains were covered over every window. It was dark, musty and there were webs hanging everywhere.

The girls looked through different boxes to find out what was stored in them. As they searched around Patty came across some old photographs of her ancestors. She wondered who they were. They wore old fashioned clothes and hairdos. Selma found some old jewelry in another box. The girls were amazed at what they found up in the attic of their parents' home.

Patty and Selma continued to search in more boxes for more things. They came across some Indian dolls dressed in Indian clothes and Indian jewelry which appeared hundreds of years old.

After the girls left the attic they decided to ask their parents about what they found in the attic. Patty's mother said the photographs were taken at least one hundred years ago of her great-grandparents and other earlier relatives. The Indian dolls had been saved by previous relatives.

Patty and Selma occasionally explored in the attic on rainy days when they were trapped in the house on rainy days with little to do. They were fascinated with the things they found!

# THIRTY-THREE

## *SCAVENGERS EXIST*

Scavengers exist around the world. Scavengers may be birds, as well as other animals. Common scavengers are vultures. Vultures smell blood and dead flesh for many miles away. They fly for many miles to places where wild animals have been killed and are lying on the ground in the open.

Vultures eat up scraps and old, decayed animals. They clean up the environment when they eat leftovers on a regular basis.

Hyenas are scavengers in the savannahs of Africa. They group together to search for hunted leftovers from other meat-eating African animals. They clean up the remainders of carcasses and leftover, animal flesh.

Hippopotami eat everything in sight in swamps and swamplands. They have large mouths and big teeth. They can be dangerous when human beings approach their swamps and swamplands. They are known to attack unexpectedly and suddenly without any warning.

Some primitive, human tribes are cannibals. They eat

available, dead flesh in order to survive. They must eat what is available in their jungle and desert surroundings.

Scavengers are needed on Earth to clean up debris and dead matter. Dead carcasses and uneaten, dead flesh are not healthy to remain for insects to invade. However, certain insects also gather and eat leftovers in the wilderness. There are fewer diseases spread because scavengers clean up dead flesh and bacteria. We should appreciate scavengers for their performance to clean up the world's environment.

# THIRTY-FOUR

## *BALLROOM DANCING*

Ballroom dancing began in Austria hundreds of years ago. Ballroom dancing became popular in Paris, France and in London, England.

Ballroom dancing is a formal manner of dancing with partners and in groups. Couples are dressed in ballroom gowns for women and formal tuxedos and black suits for men. The elegant appearance of men and women is part of the ballroom experience.

Waltzes in three-four time are performed by couples. They move their feet gracefully in three-four time and four-four time. They glide across the ballroom with coordination and splendor. Fox trots and Quick Step dances are more dance steps used in ballroom dancing.

Generally a large group of couples are on the ballroom floor ready to dance. Ladies place one hand on their partners' shoulder. They hold their partners' other hand while they are dancing.

Ballroom dancing takes practice and skill in order to

maintain graceful patterns and movements. Ballroom dancing is performed in big dance halls. Generally the dance floors are very elegant and beautiful. Chandeliers may be hanging from the ceilings to add to the elegant décor of the ballroom.

Ballroom dancing still is popular especially in Austria in Europe and in Paris, France. Couples dress up to add to the grand occasion.

The Arthur Murray Studio is where participants learn different dance styles. Ballroom dancing is taught at the Arthur Murray Studios. Learning to ballroom dance takes special training and skill.

# THIRTY-FIVE

## *KEEPING AN ADDRESS BOOK*

Keeping an address book is important. An address book comes in handy so that you can look up addresses of family, friends, doctors, lawyers, banks and acquaintances, etc.

You should keep accurate addresses, phone numbers and you should update your address book. An up-to-date address book makes a difference because when you want to contact someone you know you will be able to recognize the person you want to contact.

Keep your address book in a safe, dry place. You should be able to look up birthday dates which should be listed in your address book. You will be able to send birthday cards and phone your family and friends all because you keep an up-to-date address book.

List all doctors, dentists and medical insurances, emergency numbers and community phone numbers. You should list hospitals, police, 911 and restaurant numbers, etc, in your address book to refer to when needed.

Your address book is very valuable. If you pass away other

people can refer to your address book to call everyone you know to let them know you are deceased. So, keep an address book available where you live.

# THIRTY-SIX

## *THE CHARITY DINNER*

The Atkins of Detroit, Michigan were of high society in Detroit. They were active in political and social activities in Detroit. Marlene Atkins, who was the wife of Howard Atkins, a tycoon in Michigan, decided to sponsor a charity dinner to raise money to help poverty-stricken people in Michigan.

Marlene Atkins was one of three children who grew up with luxuries, elaborate home life, plenty of food and expensive clothes. She was used to receiving abundance and everything she wanted.

Yet, Marlene was concerned about poverty-stricken children and families she observed in Detroit, Michigan. Marlene sent out invitations to many well-to-do people. She sent 1,500 invitations in the regular mail. She sent invitations to wealthy citizens throughout the whole region.

The charity dinner was on a Saturday night at 6:00 p.m. at a social club. There were 1,500 places to sit at long tables for 30 people per table. There ware 50 tables with white tablecloths draped on them. Thirty place settings were arranged on each table. Plastic flowers were on the center of each table. Twenty-five tables were indoors and twenty-five tables were outdoors.

Marlene planned a menu of delicious food for the dinner. Each dinner was $100.00. Marlene was able to collect $150,000 from the 1,500 people. Each invited dinner guest was asked to send $100.00 in advance. A dinner place was reserved for each person who paid in advance.

A sumptuous dinner consisted of roasted chicken, sliced ham, rice pilaf with mixed vegetables, steamed asparagus with cheese sauce, mixed green salad with tomatoes, olives, carrots, cucumbers with Italian dressing. Sourdough bread and butter was on each table. Whipped Jello with cream with chocolate cookies was dessert. Tea and coffee were served at each table.

The night of the charity dinner the people arrived in couples, groups and one-by-one. They were seated by the hostess at reserved places at the tables. Once everyone arrived and were seated the food was served. After dinner Marlene stood up and presented a speech to the 1,500 people.

Marlene spoke, "You were invited here tonight to enjoy this dinner. Your one hundred dollar donations are appreciated. The money will be used to help provide funds for needy people. There are many poverty-stricken people who will benefit because of this charity money."

The guests visited for a period of time during and after dinner. It was too crowded for dancing. Marlene didn't arrange for a band to play in order to save money. The more charity accumulated would be used to help those in need.

Marlene Atkins contributed most of the $150,000 to families in need and to homeless individuals. Some of the money was used to pay for food and rent at the social club.

Marlene continued to help needy people whenever she could. The fact that she was well off financially didn't cause her not to care about others. She continued to care about the needs of many needy people.

# THIRTY-SEVEN

## *LLAMAS FROM SOUTH AMERICA*

Llamas live in the Andes Mountains in South America. Llamas have wooly, thick hair to keep them warm in cold, winter months.

Llamas live in packs and graze on grass, wild flowers, weeds and hay. They will eat shrubs and berries. They are not meat eaters. Llamas can be trained to carry human passengers. They will cooperate as long as they are not mistreated. They spit rapidly at people who make them feel uncomfortable.

Llama hair is used for weaving into thread and yarn. Coats, sweaters, serapes, shawls, blankets and carpets are made with coarse, thick, llama hair. Llamas must adjust to being shaved at certain times of the year.

Llamas have existed for hundreds of years in the Andes Mountains. They are mammals. So they give birth to their young. Female, adult llamas produce milk for their offspring. In Peru some Peruvians drink llama milk.

Llamas can be tamed. They have hooves so they can walk up mountain trails. Llamas are valuable to the mountain people of the Andes Mountains.

# THIRTY-EIGHT

## *WEARING DARK GLASSES*

Dark glasses are used to protect our eyes from glaring sunlight. There are different shades which cause a variety of colors to respond to. Polaroid glasses are the best glasses to shield our eyes from bright sunlight and harmful sun rays.

Some dark glasses are not made with ultraviolet lenses. Dark glasses without ultraviolet lenses are harmful to wear. Many people do not know dark glasses without proper insulation to the eyes are harmful to the eyes.

Dark glasses generally have an appealing look. Tourists, movie stars as well as other people wear dark glasses.

Today reading glasses can be used with dark lenses. A person can read well with strengthened reading lenses. Dark glasses have been worn for centuries. They are useful on sunny days. Movie stars look glamorous when they wear fancy, dark glasses.

Some dark glasses are expensive while other dark glasses are inexpensive. Most people wear inexpensive, dark glasses. Wealthy people can afford expensive, dark glasses.

Dark glasses are needed in deserts and snowy regions. The sun glares very brightly in deserts and snow lands. People can become blinded by very bright sunlight. Dark glasses can protect their eyes from glaring sunlight and reflections on desert sands and in snow lands.

Dark glasses are popular to wear. People will go on wearing them as long as they are available. Be sure to select dark glasses that protect your eyes.

# THIRTY-NINE

## *THEOGENESIS REVEALED*

Theogenesis is a larger, Temple book with many lessons. Messages from Master Hilarion, Master Morya, Master Kuthumi and Master Saint Germain known as Master R and Master Jesus are presented in Theogenesis.

Laws of the Cosmos are presented in Theogenesis. The law of love, law of polarity, law of attraction and repulsion, law of reincarnation or recycling, law of balance and more laws are described in Theogenesis.

Many mystical realities can be realized once we recognize the Christ Self. Many truths and Cosmic principles are revealed to us as we search on life's pathway. The law of love helps us promote harmony and good will in our lives.

Theogenesis is approximately 750 pages. It is a New Age book of metaphysical knowledge and wisdom. In Theogenesis there are explanations for creation, correlation between mind and vehicle. Light is an impenetrable mystery. Universal mind, Universal light and Identical light exist.

Fohat, the Great Breath, permeates the Cosmos. Cosmical

electricity and magnetism operate in our Cosmos. The Fifth Breath consists as energy of cohesion. Heat, attraction and repulsion affect each other. The Fifth Breath is manas and has inner breath.

The Sixth Breath is the basis of Kryashakti. The kingdom of Divine Rhythmic Breath is Within. The Seventh Breath is Universal and illimitable. There are four lower breaths which are involved with limitations of matter.

Fohat is the principle of Sound. Ether reflects the Great Cosmic Mirror. The Seventh Breath is on the invisible plane. Mystic fire is creative force.

"Beautiful, powerful is the light which streams from the sun of this solar system. It is dwarfed into apparent insignificance by the true Light, that Light which was sent to lighten the Cosmos, the Son-Sun, the first and the last. Darkness changed instantaneously throughout the whole illimitable Cosmos into Light, white, scintillating, brilliant, inexpressible, incomprehensible and simultaneously with the birth of Light, the bringing in to manifestation by Spiritual energy the first Trinity, Breath or Motion, Sound or Will, Light or Consciousness."

"For cycles upon cycles, Light holds in its eternal bosom the forces that little by little Motion and sound were transforming – the concealed life, that at the instance of Law, would bring into the field of action those other Sons – Form, Number, Color, Sound, Cohesion, Attraction and Repulsion."

"The Light of the Central Spiritual Sun is beyond human computation. The molecular vibrations of light produce color. The atomic vibrations are sound. Each form created by the directive power of Fohat receives through the principle of form in matter."

"An organic cell is defined as a microscopic mass of matter called protoplasm, enclosing another mass of matter called the nucleus. In highly evolved cells another nucleus is found within the nucleus. The inner nucleus is termed the nucleolus."

"Every cell is a minute Cosmos in itself and obeying the laws of universal correspondence has represented in it the seven planes of being. The cell wall corresponds to the physical body. The inner lining of the cell corresponds to the lower astral body. The protoplasmic contents correspond to the vital principle – Prana. Granules scattered through the protoplasm correspond to the Kama Namus, the lower mind. Spaces (vacuoles) in the protoplasm correspond to Kama Rupa – lower desires and emotions. Nucleus corresponds to the Higher Manas or higher mind. The nucleolus corresponds to the Buddhic Principle, the Sixth Sense, from which all spiritual intuition proceeds. In the nucleolus is a radiant point or center called the centersome. This center is the synthetic Central Sun and is the point of contact with Atma which, however, is no principle, as all are synthesized in it."

"The nucleus containing the nucleolus is the Higher Ego body of the cell. The Sun is the nucleus of that Cosmical Cell we term the solar system. The Sun is therefore the Higher Ego body of our solar system of worlds. All the other parts of this Cosmic Cell can be traced to a point for point, corresponding to the parts enumerated above as the seven basic divisions."

"The planets revolving around the Sun taken collectively correspond to the lower manas, the lower ego of the solar system. The Kama Rupa Centers in the Cosmic Cell are great shifting spaces (really magnetic spheres) existing between the planets in what is called space. The nearness or remoteness of a planet to one of these great magnetic interplanetary emotional spheres can influence that planet and its humanity profoundly either physically, mentally, or morally according to the phase of activity in the sphere at that particular time. The vital principle (Prana) pervades the whole cell, definite currents circulating throughout as in any minute cell of organic tissue."

"The dependence and interdependence now having been shown between the nucleus of any cell and its other parts, we are in better position to understand the true functions of the nucleus of a cell or of a solar system. The atoms composing the nucleus are in a free state known as nascence in chemistry. In this state, atoms transmit light, heat, electricity, vital energy, gravitation, chemical action and so on. As long as the atoms remain in a free state, the radiance forced pour forth, coming primarily from Atma, contacting the nucleolus and then coursing the nucleus, and from that, as a sun-center, all through the cell."

"Now the nucleus, or the Sun, as said, is the Higher Ego body or principle of the cell and the outpour of light and heat and life always obeys the universal law of supply and demand. In other words, applying this law to the cosmical process, each planet of our system has its Lord and Master or its Higher Ego actually located in the Sun. It gives to and receives from its lower principles or self, forces, according to the law of supply and demand, and as cyclical law permits."

"Thus, if a planet and the humanity on it enters a cycle where spiritual and moral decadence occurs, those atoms in the Sun or Higher Ego body corresponding to it would be less free or become more or less materialized or condensed and transmit less life, light and other energy to that particular planet and its humanity and so a "shade" would cover the face of the Sun so far as that particular planet is concerned.

But doubtless this shade would be a simultaneous product of all the planets of any one system so that the whole Sun would be affected and darkened because of the interaction of forces mentioned."

"The Universal Mind and the Universal Monad are practically identical. But while the modern metaphysical of the western world recognizes the evident difference between the mind of one man and that of another, as a rule he does not as yet accept the teaching of the eastern mystics to the effect that this difference lies in the over or under development of a definite germ of mind stuff – Monadic essence – within the differently developed brain centers of different individuals. This germ is said to be the human Monad in contradistinction to the Divine Monad. The Divine Monad bears the same relationship to the universe as a whole that the human Monad bears to the individual man or that of the lower creations."

"The more highly developed units of the present races have reached a degree of knowledge where it has become possible to lay the foundation for the attainment of such power. The ultimate causes and effects of evolution are becoming apparent, and all their efforts toward self development should be along the lines of condensation, conservation and concentration. Altruism becomes more evident. Altruism is not a sentimental virtue. It is an absolute requisite to self development."

"Whenever any group of three or more individuals has reached a point of harmonious action of all lines of their lives, a point where perfect cooperation of will and effort obtains – a point where in fact as well as in theory they can live and act up to their highest ideals, of use and service to and for each other – they have reached a condition where it is possible for them to become an active vehicle for the spiritual forces generated by much greater beings than they have ever before been conscious of; and by becoming such a vehicle the individual evolution of each constituent part of that vehicle is carried forward by great strides."

"As previously illustrated the points of two triangles, Spirit and Matter have met and intertwined. Each such individual becomes in process of time a Savior of all those who are still beneath him in their scale of evolution. The path to the God opens wide, and instead of the slow, painful, crawling mode of procedure he has hitherto been compelled to use, he goes onward and upward as though shod with seven league boots, for he is "coming into his own" and is gaining command over the secret powers of a universe."

"The combined lights in the hearts of men have changed their Earth from a dark star, a star of light. Its blackness has been transmuted. The next evolutionary step for man has been made possible by this transmutation. The path between man and his Spiritual Father, the Regent of Mars, the Master Hilarion, has been reopened."

"Now the Word again reaches man to enable him to increase his response – to throw off the dense lethargy into which he has let himself sink – and to enable him to return to his Creator with a speed that will correspond to the Evolutionary Plan for the seventh sub-race."

"The glorious, all-powerful groups of suns which lighten the fathomless depths of space within some of the constellations, such as that surpassingly marvelous group in the constellation Hercules, which is known by astronomers as the Omega Centauri, were once but single wave motions of the ether – the ether en masse – which sprang into motion as the bidding of Infinite Law, and traveled around and throughout the etheric ocean, growing into power with every ripple and wave of their journey through worlds and systems of worlds, returning through all the kingdoms of fire, earth, air and water eventually to their starting point, as suns to lighten the great immensities, as glorious hosts possessing in themselves the power to create and sustain universes, with ability to speak the soundless, creative Word that shall send forth countless myriads of souls on the same life journey from which they returned ages and ages before."

Theogenesis is a New Age book with many messages of illumination, truth and wisdom. You can awaken to inner knowledge and higher consciousness.

# FORTY

## *ELEPHANTS STILL LIVE*

Elephants have roamed the Earth for millions of years. Presently they live in Asia and Africa. Elephants are mammals because they give birth to their young and produce milk to feed their offspring.

Elephants are very intelligent. They have good memories. As a result they can recall their experiences in the jungles and savannahs, etc. They must have enough water to drink and enough vegetation to eat. Elephants are vegetarians. They eat vegetables, foliage and fruit.

Elephants generally live in groups with their mates and offspring. A male leader of the group warns the others of dangers in the wilderness. Young elephants are protected by their mothers. Mother elephants are very protective of their offspring.

Elephants have been endangered because of elephant hunters who want ivory tusks. Elephants are shot and killed by greedy hunters who want to make money off of ivory. Elephants are becoming more extinct because of wasteful killings. They should be protected by governments where they dwell in Asia and Africa.

Some elephants are trained as workers. They learn to carry heavy logs across terrains and jungles. Some elephants perform in circuses, parades and other special events. In India they march in religious festivities. They wear fancy outfits to look well dressed and groomed to attract large crowds and audiences.

Elephants are valuable. When they are well cared for and are trained they are interesting to observe. Some elephants live in zoos around the world. They respond to human attention and affection. Some people have pet elephants that dwell in their backyards. Domesticated elephants are generally docile.

Elephant figurines are made with porcelain and glass. Elephant figurines are different sizes and are decorative. People collect them as souvenirs and display their elephant figurines in their homes.

# FORTY-ONE

## *MY HIGH SCHOOL P.E. TEACHERS*

Physical Education is required throughout high school years. I had a number of P.E. teachers in the four year program. One of my P.E. teachers was Mary Alice Mankins. She was in her late twenties when I attended high school.

Mary Alice Mankins was in excellent, physical condition. She was well coordinated and slender. Mary Alice Mankins had a sense of humor. She explained the rules and procedures for each game.

Hockey was an interesting sport. We were given rubber, knee pads to wear. Knee pads were needed so players would be able to protect their knees. Mary Alice Mankins demonstrated how to play hockey out in the field at the Arroyo Grande High School. She demonstrated how to kick the hockey ball well.

I learned to play hockey in my freshman year of high school. It was challenging to keep up with the hockey ball. I managed to kick it whenever I could. Other hockey players on the opposite team tried to get control of the ball. The object was to get the ball past the goalie to earn points for our team.

Mary Alice Mankins taught tennis at the tennis courts. We were required to wear shorts and simple, sports blouses and tennis shoes. I attempted to learn to swing my tennis racquet swiftly to hit tennis balls. I learned to hit tennis balls over the tennis net into the other tennis court.

We were given tennis partners. Our goal was to win the tennis game by hitting the tennis ball over the net again and again until the opposing team missed the tennis ball. I felt triumphant when I won tennis matches.

Basketball was another game I learned in high school. I learned to throw basketballs into the basket hoop or net. Then l learned to move about the court with other basketball players in order to get the basketball to the net in order to throw it into the basketball net (hoop) to earn points for the game. I had to learn to run swiftly and to avoid being hit by the opposite team players.

My basketball coach, Mr. Webber taught me to play basketball. He was tall and strong. He demonstrated how to throw the basketball accurately and swiftly. Mr. Webber was a very good basketball player. The basketball high school teams won many basketball games during the school year.

The football coach trained football teams. The football teams played at other high schools. Often our Arroyo Grande High School football teams won many football games. The most important football game was at Cal Poly in San Luis Obispo, California.

My brother Roland was a well known, football player at the Arroyo Grande High School. He became an accomplished football player. He helped the Arroyo Grande football team win football games.

Mr. Webber taught his football teams to be good sports. He stated, "Good sportsmanship is more important than anything else." I will remember my P.E. teachers at Arroyo Grande High School.

# FORTY-TWO

## *PENCILS AND PENS*

Pens and pencils are useful for writers and students. Often, school assignments are written with pens and pencils. Longhand assignments are written with pencils and pens.

Ballpoint pens are excellent pens to write clearly with. The ink is indelible and looks good. Other pens such as feather pens are useful. Feather pens were used centuries ago. Felt and kato pens are also used.

Bulletin board pens have thicker ink. The ink is much darker and easier to see on charts and posters. There are different, bright colors such as red, green, yellow and blue used in kato pens.

Pencils are made into different degrees of lead. There are number one, two and three pencils. Generally number two is the best pencil to write with. Pencils are used frequently in the classroom. The work done in pencil is usually dark enough to be legible. Students use pencils to do daily assignments. Lead can be used in metal pencils. Tests are completed with pencils. Students have the option to erase errors and redo assignments.

Pencils can be sharpened again and again so they can be used again and again. They are useful in the classroom and at home. Pencils are used on jobs at businesses, stores, hospitals and other places.

So, purchase some pencils and pens to use whenever you need them. They are useful especially on unexpected occasions. Some pens have lids. Other pens are pressed open. There are elegant pens and simple pens to purchase at the stores. Pens make nice gifts for relatives and friends.

# FORTY-THREE

## *THE FOREST DWELLERS*

Forest dwellers exist in many woodland regions. Rabbits, owls, squirrels, deer, bears, foxes and forest birds dwell in the forests. Robins, blue jays, wrens, woodpeckers, quail and other forest birds live in forests.

Each forest dweller has a purpose for dwelling in forests. Forests provide food and water. Trees provide shelter and protection. On warm days forests provide shade and a cooler environment for dwellers in the forest.

Deer eat leaves, stems and grass in forests. They lie down under forest trees to sleep at night. Sometimes a mother deer and her fawn hide in bushes in a forest. A bush is good camouflage to protect a fawn from danger.

Rabbits eat grass and lichen in forests. They roam around the forest floor in the shade. They settle in bushes in the forest as well as in logs. Hollow logs are places to find shelter from rain and predators.

Squirrels nest in forest branches and hollow holes in tree trunks. They gather grass and twigs to build their nests. Once the nest is built with twigs and grass squirrels settle in their hollow trunk dwelling places. They gather nuts, berries and seeds to eat.

Squirrels multiply like rabbits. Baby squirrels stay near their mothers. They dwell in hollow nests in trees. They scamper around the trees near their nest to search for nuts and grass to nibble on. Squirrels feel secure in forests. They snuggle up in their bushy tails when they sleep.

Owls dwell in forests. They sleep in branches in tall trees. At night they usually stay awake. They hoot to call to other owls. Owls have large, bright eyes. They stare at anyone that passes by as they perch on tree limbs.

Other forest birds such as robins, blue jays, wrens, woodpeckers and quail live in forests. They make their nests in trees. They eat insects in the forest. They peck for seeds on the forest floors. They are protected by shade under forest trees and in forests on grassy forest floors. Woodpeckers peck at tree trunks. They drill in holes in tree trunks and live in the holes.

We should protect forests. They hold down the soil on the Earth. They preserve the Earth and the dwellers in the forests. When we preserve our forests we preserve the life force on Earth. Forest dwellers help maintain an ecosystem in nature.

# FORTY-FOUR

## *A CAMPFIRE STORY*

The Nelsons like to go camping during warmer weather in Montana. They had packed their car for a camping excursion. They were ready to go to the national park in Montana at Yellowstone. They were able to get away from their indoor enclosure and enjoy the outdoors and fresh air.

Once the car was ready the Nelsons began their journey north to the timberland and Yellowstone National Park. The drive to Yellowstone Park was scenic and a real, adventurous journey. The pine and spruce trees were evergreen and sparkling with dewdrops because it had rained.

The Nelsons traveled over 1,000 miles to their destination at Yellowstone National Park. When they arrived at the park they drove in and located a place to camp. Molly Nelson and Fred Nelson began unpacking the car. They had been married ten years. Camping was one of their interests. They generally went camping at least once a year.

Fred unpacked tents and began assembling two of them. The second tent was for their children. Ted was eight years old and Selena was six years old. They would share a tent during this camping trip. Fred asked Ted to assist him in setting up the tents.

Fred took tent stakes and hammered stakes in a square area in the ground. Fred took tend canvas and tied the canvas to string and to the stakes to hold the canvas up. Once the canvas was in place and tied securely each tent was ready to use.

Molly unpacked food and cooking equipment. She dug a hold in the ground. She asked Selena to help put small logs in the hole for a campfire. Molly placed some paper over the logs and dry brush from the campground. She began a campfire.

Molly placed a large metal grill over the campfire. Pots and pans could be placed on this grill in order to cook. Molly cleaned some potatoes, carrots and string beans. She filled a pot with water and placed it on the grill over the campfire. She boiled the potatoes, carrots and string beans in the pot. She added baby corn, squash and sliced tomatoes in the pot. Then Molly cut up some slices of beef. She added the beef to the cooking vegetables. Molly added herbs and salt and pepper to the beef vegetable stew.

Selena watched the stew cooking in the pot. Molly asked Selena to butter some bread and pour milk into glasses. There was a picnic table at the campsite to sit at for meals. Molly and Selena set the table. Selena put the buttered bread on the table. She placed glasses of milk on the table at each place setting.

When the beef stew was cooked and ready to eat Molly, Fred, Selena and Ted sat down to enjoy it. The stew tasted delicious. They ate the buttered bread and drank the cold milk. While they were eating they heard birds chirping in the nearby pine trees. There were some white puffy clouds in the sky.

The breeze began to blow. It was late Spring. Yet, the wind was cold. Selena and Molly felt cold. Molly got up from the table to locate warm jackets for Selena, Ted, Fred and herself. She brought jackets to her family. Everyone bundled up in their jackets to warm up.

The Nelsons could see snow-capped mountains in the distance. The geysers at Yellowstone National Park were within a few miles from the campsite. Bears were known to roam through the national park. Deer and rabbits were moving about in different locations in the national park.

After the Nelsons finished their evening meal Molly and Selena washed and dried the dishes and cooking equipment. Fred and Ted took out bedrolls and warm blankets and put them in the tents. They smoothed the ground in the tents so the tent floors would be comfortable to walk on.

Before bedtime Molly, Fred, Selena and Ted sat around the campfire which was still burning. The campfire was warm and cozy in the night air. Fred spoke to his family. He asked, "Would you like to hear a story?" Selena's eyes lit up and she looked eager and excited to hear a story. Ted seemed interested in hearing his father tell a story. Molly said, "We would love to hear a story."

So, Fred began telling a story. He said, "Once when I was camping near the Rocky Mountains I camped near a thick, evergreen forest. I explored the region and gathered logs and brush to use for a campfire. As I wandered through the forest of tall, shady evergreen trees I saw owls perched in high branches. The owls were hooting. Their eyes were bright. They stared at me as I walked by. I wasn't afraid of the hooting owls. I continued strolling in the forest. It was mid afternoon."

Fred continued telling his story. He said, "As I was walking along I came to a big, fallen tree log. I decided to look into a hollow section of the big, dead log. Suddenly I saw several red foxes lying in the log. They were sleeping. They heard me and woke up. They were frightened when they saw me. They quickly ran out of the hollow log to get away from me. I had no intention of harming them. Because they were wild they ran away to be sure they would be safe. I continued walking deeper in the forest. I heard many sounds of insects and birds. Suddenly, a big, black bear approached me unexpectedly. It was enormous and it stood on its hind legs. It gritted its teeth and glared at me with its piercing eyes."

Fred tried to remain calm as he continued to tell his story. He continued. "The big, black bear started walking closer to me on its hind legs. I became very nervous and frightened. I didn't have a gun with me. I only had a pocket knife to defend myself. I stopped quickly in my tracks. I knew that if I made the wrong move or decision the bear could kill me. I decided to walk slowly away as calmly as possible. The bear stood there without moving. I decided to climb the nearest, tall tree. I quickly got up on a branch and continued to climb up the tree. The bear got on all four feet and ran over to the tree. It reached up to try to grab me. Fortunately, I was able to climb to the top of the sturdy tree. I managed to get out my pocket knife to use in case the bear came too close."

Fred continued his story. "The bear shook the tree I was in. I held on tight so I wouldn't fall out of the tree. I cut twigs off the tree. I threw them at the big bear after making sharp points on them. I threw one twig at a time at the bear. I waited for quite some time for the bear to give up. It was getting dark. The moon came out. Moonlight was gleaming in the forest."

"When early morning came the bear finally ran off. I was relieved that the bear gave up and left the area. I waited for another fifteen minutes to be sure it didn't reappear. I climbed slowly down the tree and reached the ground. Once I was on the ground I headed back to my camp which was southeast. I finally returned to my campsite. My car was locked and parked near the campsite. My tent was still intact. The campfire was unused because I had spent the night in the forest. I decided to leave the area. I didn't want to encounter any more bears. I headed home which was hundreds of miles away. I thought about how fierce and dangerous the big, black bear was. I was grateful to be safe and unharmed." Fred was finished with his story.

Molly responded. "Whooh! What an experience you had." Ted said, "Are there big, black bears where we are now?" Fred replied, "Bears live at Yellowstone National Park. So, be alert and watch out for bears!" Selena spoke. "I am afraid of bears!" Molly responded, "Don't worry Selena. We will keep a campfire blazing all night. If we keep our food packed safely in the trunk of our car this will help keep bears away."

Fred realized that he had aroused his family by telling them about the big, black bear he had encountered near the Rocky Mountains. He said, "I have a gun in case we have any bears roam near our campground. I will sit up and watch over our campground. So, don't worry. It is getting dark. Go to bed and get a good night's sleep."

Molly, Selena and Ted decided to go to bed. They entered their tents and got in their bedrolls after they zipped their tents. Fred sat down near a big tree near the campsite to guard the campground. He tried to stay awake. He kept the fire blazing all night.

Around 3:00 a.m. in the morning Fred fell asleep at the tree. The fire was still blazing. Fred kept his gun near him in case he needed to use it. Suddenly a big, brown bear wandered into the camp. It moved in the brush and twigs making noises. Fred woke up in time. He saw the big, brown bear roaming near the car. He took his gun and aimed it at the bear. The bear turned and saw Fred. Fred cocked his gun and shot the bear four or five times until it fell on the ground and appeared dead. Fred inspected the bear carefully. It was dead.

Molly, Selena and Ted came out of their tents and saw the big, brown bear lying dead on the ground. They were amazed at its size. Molly went over and hugged her husband, Fred. She said, "Thanks for protecting us. This bear could have hurt us!" Fred looked at his wife, Molly. He was still feeling upset about having to kill the bear. He said, "I killed the bear. I didn't want to risk our lives. Bears are unpredictable!" Selena came over and hugged her father. She said, "Daddy, you are brave." Ted said, "Dad, you did the right thing. Don't worry about it. We are all safe, thanks to your prompt decision to kill the bear. Thanks for protecting us!" Fred felt better because his wife and children were so supportive.

# FORTY-FIVE

## *OFFICE CHATTER*

Working in an office requires acceptance and understanding of other office workers. Certain office skills should be learned such as filing business papers, answering telephones, typing business letters, mimeographing business papers, etc.

Workers in an office share specific responsibilities and social obligations. Office workers get to know one another over a period of time. As workers become more and more acquainted they communicate more effectively. They tend to become more personable as they find out about their lives.

Gossip is a common occurrence in many offices. Workers gossip about their co-workers. They may talk about mistakes and errors co-workers make. Co-workers may discuss marriage problems with other workers. They chatter about personal problems and relationships with different people. Once these workers become informed about personal problems and relationships the details are revealed often to other co-workers during coffee breaks and lunch time.

One day Silvia Jensen went to lunch with two of her

office co-workers. They went to a local restaurant next door to order their lunches. Silvia ordered a shrimp salad and clam chowder. Jean Murphy, another office worker, ordered a cheeseburger with fries. Nina Henderson, another office worker, ordered a tuna sandwich with potato salad. They all ordered iced tea to drink with their lunch.

While the three office workers were waiting for their lunches they had time to chatter about anything they wanted to talk about. Silvia began talking about her cousin. Alice was planning to get married in a month. Silvia was excited about her cousin's chance to marry someone she loved. Jean and Nina listened to Silvia describe the details of the wedding arrangements. Her cousin Alice was going to wear a white, taffeta, embroidered, long dress and white, half heels. Her bridesmaids would be wearing lavender gowns with white flowers and white high heels. The invitations had been sent out to over one hundred people. The wedding would take place in a beautiful garden at the Unitarian Church. Silvia was excited about this special occasion.

Jean decided to talk about a new worker in the office by the name of Ellen Corby. Jean said, "Ellen is coming in late frequently. I have to do some of her work so it will be done on time! She shouldn't be late constantly. She also works too slow! I shouldn't have to do her work!" Silvia replied, "Have you spoken to her about being late?" Jean answered, "Yes. She still walks in at least a half hour late!" Silvia responded, "You should tell the manager about this." Jean said, "I intend to tell the manager. The new worker may lose her job."

Nina spoke, "I have noticed that Ellen is late frequently." Jean said, "Maybe we both can tell the manager about Ellen's lateness." The food was brought to the table by the waitress and placed according to each order. More iced tea was poured in each glass. The three women began eating their lunch. The food was appetizing and light.

As they ate lunch Silvia, Jean and Nina talked about their jobs. They were concerned about some of the working conditions. Jean said, "My morning coffee break is too short! I only get fifteen minutes for time to go to the bathroom. I have to take coffee back to my desk and sip on it while I am working."

Nina responded, "We all get fifteen minutes for a coffee break in the mornings. I don't have time to enjoy a real break either. At least we get forty-five minutes at lunch time. We have around twenty-five minutes left before we have to be back at work."

Silvia spoke. "The time is divided up. Fifteen minutes for two coffee breaks a day and forty-five minutes for lunch. We get seventy-five minutes a day for breaks. We are here from 8:30 a.m. to 5:00 p.m. I guess the thirty minutes before work is the reason why coffee breaks are shorter. If we came in at 8:00 a.m. then maybe we could have longer coffee breaks. I think I will talk to the manager about coming in at 8:00 a.m. Maybe we will have more time for our breaks."

The women finished their lunches. They had chattered about their concerns. Now it was time to return to the office so they wouldn't be late. They paid for the lunches and left a fifteen percent tip. Then they walked next door to their office to continue with their work at 1:00 p.m. to 5:00 p.m.

# FORTY-SIX

## *MOVIE AND STAGE PLAY GOERS*

People still go out to see movies at theaters. High school and college students go to theaters more than other age groups. They go on dates. Attending theaters are a popular form of entertainment. Theaters are places for couples, families and groups of people to go to be together.

Many new movies are coming out every year. There are family dramas, adventure movies, western, murder mysteries, romantic episodes, human interest, historical and science fiction films. Some movies become Academy Award movies.

People still enjoy viewing up-to-date movies on large screens in theaters. During intermission theater goers go to the refreshment stand to select popcorn, candy and hot dogs. They return to the theater to see the next movie or the second half of a longer movie.

Theaters will probably always be available. As long as films are produced movie producers will send their movies to different theaters around the country. Theater tickets are sold before each movie starts. Tickets range in price according to age groups. Senior citizens generally receive a discount for each show.

Stage plays are still popular especially in big cities. Broadway shows are presented in New York City. Stage plays are performed downtown and at colleges. Melodrama in Oceano, California has been open over twenty-five years. Many people still go to this Melodrama theater. Popcorn, cold drinks and beer are served at the Melodrama Theater in Oceano.

In San Luis Obispo, California there are several stage play theaters. Refreshments are served during intermission. Stage plays have different acts and scenes. Sets and props are changed as the plays are performed. Costumes are changed in between acts and at intermission. Stage plays are different than films. There are far less scenes in stage plays. Sets and props are limited in stage plays. The same set may be use frequently based on the action in the plays.

Santa Maria CPH Theater is well known at Allen Hancock College. Many well known plays and musicals are performed at this popular theater. Tickets are usually purchased in advance. They vary in price. The stage is larger in the college theater. There are at least 2,000 seats in this theater.

People will continue to go to movies and stage plays as long as they exist. Prices may vary from year to year. Going to the theater is still a popular event.

# FORTY-SEVEN

## *ELECTRICITY COUNTS*

Electricity is an important form of energy. Electricity was discovered several hundred years ago by Benjamin Franklin when he used a metal key in a kite. Lightning hit the metal key in the kite. The kite lit up with light.

Thomas Edison invented the first light bulbs. The bulbs had filters and voltage generated in watts to create light. Different light bulb sizes were created so there were 40 watts, 60 watts, 75 watts and more as light bulbs were produced.

Electric lights make a difference. We can see much better at night and in windowless rooms. Nicholas Tesla, who was from Poland, discovered the used of alternating electrical current. More light could be produced with alternating current electricity.

General Electric Company was formed by Thomas Edison. With electricity we can have many electrical appliances in our homes such as toasters, irons, microwave ovens, roasters, lamps, ceiling lights and many more items.

With electricity we can travel farther. Electric cars are

now being produced in the world. Many household items and toys are made with electricity. Office equipment such as computers, electric typewriters and mimeograph machines and household items such as refrigerators and stoves use electricity. Electricity is a valuable source of energy.

# FORTY-EIGHT

## *CANDLELIGHT SERVICES*

Candlelight services are sacred and very special. Candlelight services are held in churches and temples. Many candles are lit on altars and tables. Candlelight creates a special effect in chapels and cathedrals.

Acolytes in the Catholic Church march up the main aisle in twos while they carry candles to the altar. The light from candles symbolize the sacred light of God. Flames of freedom exist in candlelight.

Special ceremonies take place in which each person who comes to participate, receives a candle which is lit during the ceremony. Each person repeats certain, sacred words while the candles are lit around a circle. Candlelight services may take place whenever religious leaders choose to have them. Each participant is allowed to keep his or her candle.

# FORTY-NINE

## *THE GARDEN PARTY*

Florence Heely lived in a scenic neighborhood where there were large, magnificent homes and gardens. She was fairly new to this neighborhood. She took pride in her colorful garden.

Florence spent a lot of time working in her garden. She planted dahlias, daisies, geraniums, roses, asters and some irises. She cultivated her garden, pulled out weeds and watered her garden.

Since Florence was new to the town she decided to have a garden party. It was nearly summertime. Flowers were blossoming everywhere. Green grass and four-leaf clovers were growing abundantly in the area. Florence wanted to become acquainted with her neighbors.

Invitations were sent out to all the nearby neighbors. Florence also called some neighbors to be sure they attended her garden party.

Florence prepared finger sandwiches, cookies, cake, sliced, fresh fruit such as strawberries, blueberries and banana slices.

She placed paper plates, plastic silverware and napkins on a garden table. She prepared hot tea and coffee as well as fruit punch.

The garden party was at 2:00 p.m. on Tuesday afternoon. Florence had all refreshments ready for her guests. Neighbors began to arrive at 2:00 p.m. on. Florence greeted each neighbor as he or she arrived. The garden party was in the back yard where Florence had cultivated a beautiful flower garden.

Each invited guest visited with other guests. Many of the neighbors knew each other. So they were able to visit with each other. Florence mingled among her invited guests and spoke to them in a friendly manner. Around twenty guests arrived to participate at the garden party.

Refreshments were served to each guest. The neighbors stood around eating refreshments while they spoke to on another. Florence found out that some of her neighbors had lived in the neighborhood for over twenty-five years or more. Some neighbors had lived there at least ten years. Florence was the newest person in the neighborhood. She hoped to make new friends in her new neighborhood.

Florence came from a Latino background. She could speak four languages fluently. She was a versatile person. She was capable of communicating effectively about a variety of topics. She hoped to be accepted in the neighborhood.

The garden party was over at 4:15 p.m. Florence was able to speak to many of her neighbors. She talked about politics, social issues and gardening. She made a good impression on her neighbors. The fact that she invited them to her home to enjoy a garden party made a difference.

# FIFTY

## *BEVERLY SILLS,*
## *A FAMOUS OPERA STAR*

Beverly Sills, a well known opera star was born in 1929. "Brilliant at all levels of her vocal range, she has a particularly exquisite coloratura, crystalline, strong, flexible and always pitch perfect." In addition, she is a magnificent actress, who has taken many unusual roles assigned to coloratura sopranos. She has turned these roles into even more exciting dramatic situations.

Among Beverly Sills' triumphs are Pamira in Rossini's Siege of Corinth, which she revived at La Scala after a 116 year lapse. Lucia in Donizetti's Lucia di Lammermoor, which Beverly Sills introduced in a new production in 1969 with her home company, a New York City Opera and Cleopatra in Handel's Julius Caesar.

Beverly Sills began singing at age three when she became a singer on a children's radio program called Uncle Ben's Rainbow House. Then she sang with Major Bowes and then later performed as a mountain girl on a soap opera Our Gal

<u>Sunday</u>. Beverly Sills' big hit was the originator of the Rinso White jingle, one of radio's first singing commercials.

After graduation from high school in 1945 at the age of 15, Beverly Sills began ten years as an apprentice, traveling singer, doing everything from Sigmund Romberg to Gilbert and Sullivan in many American towns between Miami and San Diego.

In 1955 Beverly Sills joined the New York City Opera. She received training there for a period of time. After years of more hard work developing role after role she finally began in 1966 and 1967 to receive recognition. The years of hard work have paid off handsomely, not only in making her one of the great singers of her decade but also in giving her the perspective and good sense that have made her a compassionate, human being.

# FIFTY-ONE

## *THE IMPORTANCE OF EARLY CHILDHOOD EDUCATION*

Early childhood education has become an important concern in modern times. The earlier a child begins to learn about his or her environment, social situations and early skills will help a child grow and develop more effectively.

An inquisitive child asks questions and is eager to find out about happenings and experiences around him or her. Inquisitive children want to know such things as why is the sky blue? Why does the Sun product light? Why are we here? Why does the Earth move around the Sun?

If children are surrounded with stimulating materials such as tangible items he or she will generally learn to use these educational materials. Place puzzles, blocks, maps, miniature animals, folded napkins, clay, geometric objects, etc, on shelves. Allow children to select what they want to learn about. Most children will be eager to learn to use these tangible materials.

It is important to encourage children to ask questions.

The more inquisitive they are the more they can learn at an earlier age. What kinds of experiences encourage growth? What kinds of experiences inhibit growth? Can these results be changed?

Many disadvantaged children need to be given the opportunity to learn at an early age. If children are placed in a creative, stimulating environment they have a much better opportunity to grow and learn.

The newly vigorous faith in early childhood education has been rapidly popularized. Students studying to be teachers are required to take Early Childhood Education courses when they major in Elementary Education. An understanding and awareness of children's needs is important.

Children who are provided with knowledge, instructions and guidance at an early age develop much better. They learn to adapt to their environment much better. Children eager to learn are healthier and usually more well adjusted to life at an earlier age.

In 1964 <u>Stability And Change In Human Characteristics</u> by Benjamin S. Bloom, professor of education at the University of Chicago, was published. He was a scholar for scholars. This book was not a casual book for laymen. "After pouring over more than a thousand longitudinal studies of human growth in the past half century, Bloom began to uncover certain regularities of human development. For every characteristic he found there was a typical growth curve. Half of a child's future height is usually reached by the age of two years and six months. Half of a male's aggressiveness is established by the age of three. Half of a person's intelligence is developed by the age of four. Thirty percent more of an individual's total intellectual growth occurs between the ages of four and eight. Thus, half of a child's intellectual development takes place before the school ever sees him and eighty percent has occurred by the time he finished second or third grade."

Furthermore, Bloom found it is during this phase of rapid development when a characteristic is least stable, that the environment can have the greatest impact. For example, malnutrition does not affect the height of an 18-year-old but can greatly retard the growth of an infant, and such a loss in the early years can never be fully made up.

The environment shapes the cognitive growth of the infant and young child. The child gains his first knowledge of himself and the world from the stimuli provided by his surroundings and because of these perceptions he begins to construct his universe.

Through the work of the Swiss psychologist Jean Piaget, we can watch the young human being grow from his first grasping motions to the "age of reason." From the very start, the infant's reflex patterns are shaped by interaction with the outside world.

At five months a baby learns to coordinate his senses of touch, sight, sound and motion in order to make things happen deliberately. He learns to reach and grasp things, to rattle the mobile over his crib and to throw his toys. He begins to distinguish between himself and the outside world.

Soon a toddler will learn to find his toys when they are missing. Once he grasps what Piaget calls the concept of the permanent object, once he realized that the toy continues to exist even though he cannot see it, then he can begin to relate to the world in a consistent fashion and begin to investigate his environment aggressively. By the time language begins, the child has already acquired a formidable range of knowledge.

The important Piaget places on these sensorimotor operations is corroborated by biologists who have found that such activity permanently affects the chemistry and anatomy of the brain.

The effect of isolation and lack of attention and activity on children in their first years can be seen in studies of infants raised in orphanages where they are fed and bathed but otherwise neglected. Without toys and with minimal contact with adults such youngsters can be severely retarded. Orphans in Tehran grew so apathetic that fewer than half of them learned to sit up alone by the age of two, a feat usually accomplished by ten months. At the age of four many had not learned to walk.

Until recently child psychologists blamed such tragedies solely on lack of mother love. But cognitive psychologists believe the problem stems less from the infants' separation from their mothers than from the dullness of their surroundings. They lie all day on white-sheeted mattresses, surrounded by protective white bumpers on their cribs, and stare at a blank ceiling. Nobody talks to them. They have no toys. They even take their nourishment alone from bottles propped up for them. Babies in such institutions keep waiting for something interesting to happen.

Burton L. White of Harvard University decided to experiment with babies in a hospital nursery. He discovered that babies given attention, proper nourishment and a stimulating environment were more alert and they learned faster and developed much sooner. Toddlers learned to walk and talk better and sooner. A stimulating environment makes a difference in the development and growth of children stage by stage.

# FIFTY-TWO

## *PARAPSYCHOLOGY*

In 1893, Hans Berger, who later recorded his first human electroencephalogram, had an experience that inspired him to study the interactions between mental phenomena and physiological processes.

One day Hans Berger was almost in an accident with a horse when he fell off the horse on a ledge. He thought about the possible accident that he narrowly escaped. However, his thoughts about this accidental occurrence were transmitted to his sister through telepathy because he was close to his sister.

The first reports of telepathy date back when primitive people dreamed about unobserved events, rituals that involved the apparently successful prediction of future happenings and meditative procedures that were said to produce direct effects on distant objects. These occurrences may have been instances of what parapsychologists (those who study them) now label telepathy, clairvoyance, precognition and psychokinesis – the four types of so-called psi phenomena which probably still conjure up images of tea leaves and crystal balls.

Uri Geller was capable of bending spoons, keys, rings and other metal objects seemingly by sheer concentration. The Parapsychological Association, the professional organization for such researchers, has been admitted to affiliate membership in the American Association for the Advancement of Science, one of many indications that the existence of extrasensory perception (ESP) and psychokinesis is now gaining much wider acceptance in the scientific and scholarly communities.

Sigmund Freud expressed a cautious interest in psi, suggesting that personality psychodynamics could unconsciously distort telepathic messages in dreams. Another founder of psychoanalysis, Carl Gustav Jung, was fascinated by psi phenomena throughout his professional life. He hypothesized the existence of a "collective unconscious," serving as the foundation for each individual's psi experiences. Other psychoanalysts who have described clinical case histories thought to have a psi component include Jan Ehrenwold, Jule Eisenbred, Emilio Servadio and Montague Ullman.

The Society for Psychical Research was founded in London in 1882. This first major organization was created to attempt the scientific assessment of psi. This society attracted the attention of many distinguished scholars. The most active participants included the philosopher Henry Sedgwick, the physicist Sir William Barrett and the classist Frederic W.H. Myers. William James, philosopher and psychologist, established the American Society for Psychical Research.

In 1884 the probability theory was the first applied to the assessment of deviations from theoretically expected chance outcomes by the French physiologist Charles Richet, a Nobel laureate in ESP experiments involving card guessing. The most extensive use of card guessing procedures was initiated at Duke University in the late 1920s and early 1930s by William McDougall, the eminent Anglo-American psychologist and others – notably J.B. Rhine, A McDougall protégé, and L.E. Rhine, his wife.

The first Duke experiments employed an ESP deck of 25 cards divided equally among five suits with each suit having its own symbol. It could be predicted from the laws of probability that, on the average, five correct guesses as to the symbol on the card would be made by a subject on each run through the deck. Better than chance scores were considered to provide evidence of ESP.

Telepathy was generally tested by having a person in one room guess the order of cards as they were observed in another room by an agent or transmitter. Testing for clairvoyance involved having a subject guess the order of cards as they lay face down. The Rhines carried on this work after McDougall's death and initiated precognition experiments in which subjects tried to anticipate the future order of the cards in an ESP deck about to be shuffled or otherwise randomized.

The most highly publicized early experiment was a clairvoyance test in which one Hubert Pearce, a Duke University student attempted to guess symbols on individual cards handled by an experimenter in another building. A total of 1,850 guesses were made over a seven month period in 1933 and 1934. 558 were correct guesses or hits, about fifty percent more than the 370 hits that would have been predicted by probability theory. And according to the laws of probability, such a success will occur only once every 22 billion trials.

J.B. Rhine published his first major work, <u>Extrasensory Perception</u> in 1934. the major issue concerned the validity of the assumption that the probability of success in the card guessing experiments was actually one in five. B.H. Camp, president of the Institute of Mathematical Statistics, approved the Rhines' evaluative techniques. When J.B. Rhine initiated the Journal of Parapsychology in 1937 he employed a statistician to check the mathematics in each article before it was published.

By 1940 the Rhines and their colleagues had reported thirty-three experiments involving nearly one million experimental trials, under conditions they were certain precluded sensory leakage. The results were statistically significant in 27 of the 33.

Photographers that scores remained at the chance level. The believer's score sheet showed results that were higher than chance, while the nonbeliever's sheet showed results that were lower.

Gardner Murphy, an eminent American psychologist who was also a pioneer in Parapsychology, analyzed 175,000 trials from actual ESP experiments, finding only 0.10 percent errors. It has generally been concluded that scoring errors alone could not account for the Rhines' astronomically high levels of statistical significance.

Anyone who conducts parapsychological experiments needs to bear in mind that chances vary and accurate accountings may not always exist. Parapsychology is the study of extrasensory phenomena or psi. It is sometimes called psychical research. Psi is all extrasensory interactions between organisms and their external environment including other organisms. Extrasensory perception (ESP) is any acquisition of information without use of the senses. It includes clairvoyance, precognition and telepathy.

# FIFTY-THREE

## *TORONTO, A COSMOPOLITAN CITY*

Toronto, Canada is a booming, cosmopolitan city with a population of over 4 million people today. It has preserved a unique, neighborhood look even though Toronto continues to expand and grow.

In 1985 Toronto celebrated its 150th anniversary. Many people gathered at the harbor in Toronto to celebrate this memorable anniversary. At one time Toronto was called York after the Duke of York. Toronto as well as five other urban cities, Etobicoke, Scarborough, York, East York and North York are near Lake Ontario.

This location and the excellent natural harbor it provides have been largely responsible for Toronto's emergence as Canada's financial, commercial and industrial center. Toronto is a distribution place for goods produced in the surrounding region.

In 1983 approximately 3,067,100 people lived in metro Toronto. Over one million people live in the city of Toronto today. Toronto is clean and beautiful. Toronto owes much of its success to the careful planning that went into its development in the past decades. The city began to boom after World War II when many people came from Europe and from other places.

Hundreds of high-rise apartments sprang up everywhere during the 1960s to supply incoming immigrants. Toronto became recognized as one of the pioneers of neighborhood protection. The developers learned to work with the zoning code.

One notable project began in 1970 when Toronto's historic waterfront was revised on Lake Ontario. Located at the southern edge of the downtown area, the waterfront now includes the 92 acre Harbourfront, offering a wide variety of restaurants, art exhibits and entertainment, as well as the new Queen's Quay Terminal, a blending of condominiums, offices, shops and a dance theater. The entire location has experienced a renaissance in recent years and now boasts three miles of climate-controlled underground walkways with hundreds of shops, cafes and gardens.

The CN Tower in Toronto which is 1,815 feet high is the world's tallest freestanding structure. It was completed in 1975 on the tract itself. In 1980 work began on a 20,000 capacity convention center in the shadow of the CN Tower on the fringe of the railway land. The center and an adjoining hotel opened in the fall of 1984. the Royal Bank of Canada opened a new computer center on the northern edge of the tract in 1985.

In December 1983 the Toronto City Council approved a development concept outlining the general plan for the railway land project. Toronto sketches its recorded history back to 1615 when Etienne Brule, an interpreter for the French explorer, Samuel de Champlain, became the first white man to see the huge inland Lake Ontario at the mouth of what is now the Humber River. Brule was told by Mississauga Indians that the area was called "Toronto," an Indian word meaning meeting place.

A small fur-trading outpost was established at Toronto in 1720 but the French didn't take any interest in this area until 1749 when they established the tiny Fort Rouille on what is now the grounds of the Canadian National Exhibition, a huge annual fair. After the British victory in the French and Indian War, Britain gained control of all of Canada in 1763. Toronto began to take on increased importance under English rule. In 1787 the British officially bought the site from the Mississuagas for 1,700 pounds in cash.

Colonel John Graves Simcoe became the first British lieutenant governor of the province, which was then called Upper Canada. Toronto, which became the province capital in 1793, was named York in honor of the Duke of York. Toronto moved forward even in its slower years. By 1844, the population had grown to 18,420.

King's College, the forerunner of the University of Toronto, was built in the 1840s. The St. Lawrence Hall, still standing today, opened in 1850 as the social and cultural center of Toronto. By the 1850s Toronto developed the first railway serving the city. Toronto soon became a major commercial and manufacturing center.

When the Dominion of Canada was born in 1867, the population of Toronto was 45,000. the expanding railway system allowed Toronto to serve a huge area, and the city grew to 208,000 people as Toronto stepped quickly into the 20th Century.

Toronto was the home for different celebrities such as Mary Pickford, a motion picture actress knows as America's

Sweetheart. She was born on University Avenue. Christopher Plummer, Beatrice Lillie, Raymond Massey and composer Percy Faith, pianist Glenn Gould, opera star Gordon Lightfoot all lived in Toronto. Singer Anne Murray lived north of Metro in Toronto.

Sir Sandford Fleming introduced the concept of standard time in 1884, and Canada Dry Ginger Ale was developed in 1904. Also in 1904 five-pin bowling, the most popular form of bowling in Canada, was invented by a Torontonian entrepreneur when the patrons at his bowling alley could not complete a regular game during their lunch break.

One of Canada's most important artists, Tom Thompson, lived in a little shack in the downtown Rosedale Ravine. Associated with Thompson were the Group of Seven painters of Canada's national scene, which had its first show at the Art Gallery of Toronto on May 7, 1920.

Years ago Toronto was mainly Anglo-Saxon in origin. However, the population has grown increasingly. Today Metro in Toronto has the largest Italian, Portuguese and Jewish communities in Canada. There is a large, black population, strong Chinese and German communities and many people of Indo-Pakistani, Greek, Ukrainian, Hispanic, Polish, Hungarian, Filipino, Baltic, Korean, Maltese, Yugoslav and Arabic origin. Although English remains the principal language in Toronto almost one-third of Metro residents have different, mother tongues.

Because Toronto has become a cosmopolitan city there are a variety of restaurants and types of cuisines available. There were only French restaurants in Toronto until the different restaurants came into existence. Today there are hundreds of restaurants. There is a bustling Chinatown, a Greek area, an Italian section and a Jewish area all offering traditional foods.

Toronto celebrated its cultural and ethnic diversity in 1984 in June. They featured pavilions around the city offering different types of food, drink and entertainment. The West Indian community in late July and early August held Caribana with a dance festival, a carnival and a huge picnic.

Some 20 million people visit Toronto each year. In 1984 the entire city got involved in a celebration known as Sesqui. The City Hall sported a giant birthday cake to welcome visitors including Queen Elizabeth II of Britain and Pope John Paul II, both of whom arrived in September, 1984.

Several days at the end of June and the beginning of July were set aside to celebrate Canada's official birthday. Special events took place such as Canada's Wonderland, a Disneyland type theme park eight miles north of Metro Toronto's boundaries. The province of Ontario hosted another birthday party on July 1 on the lawns of Queen's Park, the historic, old capitol building with five-cent hot dogs, soft drinks and a full morning and afternoon of entertainment by local entertainers and performers. Later in July, millions welcomed the historic sailing vessels called the Tall Ships at Lake Ontario.

Toronto is a city with many attractions. The largest tourist attraction is the downtown Eaton Centre, a huge, multilevel, shopping mall which is modeled after Milan's Galleria in which live many birds who fly among the fountains, the trees and the greenery. Behind the Eaton Centre is the CN Tower with its revolving restaurants, discos and two observation levels. Many views far away can be seen from the observation area.

The Metro Toronto Zoo covers 710 rolling acres northeast of the city. It is one of the largest zoos in the world. There are fifty miles of public beaches within Metro. In the summer people may board one of the three old ferries for a ten minute trip across the harbor to the Toronto Islands, five islands with public beaches, parks, picnic areas and a small amusement park.

# FIFTY-FOUR

## *THE LOUVRE IN PARIS, FRANCE*

Once a palace, the Louvre has evolved into the world's larges, art museum in Paris, France. Its rich, extensive collections encompass classical Egyptian and Near Eastern antiquities and centuries of Western paintings, drawings, sculptures and decorative arts.

The expansion and reorganization of the Louvre is aimed at displaying this wealth of art to the world. The Louvre once was a fortress. King Charles I, who ascended the French throne in 1364 decided to make the old fortress more attractive in the 14th Century.

Francis I returned to France from wars and captivity in Italy in the late 1520s. The history of the present Louvre begins with the design and construction of Francis' Renaissance. He wanted a true palace constructed with artistry and refinement. So he tore down the old tower and built a palace. Pierre Lescot was the architect who designed the new palace which eventually became the Louvre.

The Louvre as it now stands is the outcome of a plan that

evolved somewhat randomly. It involved both the Louvre palace itself and the adjacent Palais des Tuileries built in the 1560s for Catherine de Medicis, widow of Henry II, as a country house outside the city walls. During the 19th Century the last kings of France lived in the Tuileries Palace.

The current Louvre museum's endless Grande Galerie du Bord de l'Eau (great gallery on the riverside), which presents a marathon challenge, was the result of a desire, shared by a succession of kings, to connect these two palaces.

The Louvre palace was not used as a royal residence after 1682 when Louis XIV moved the court to Versailles. Its career as a museum began in 1793, when former royal collections were opened to the public during the French Revolution.

A new Louvre was established in 1986 to allow expansion of the museum which was made by President Mitterand in 1981. A former director of French museums, George Salles, once remarked that the Louvre was like a "theater without wings." Fifty percent of the floor space in the Louvre is used for storage, workshops, laboratories, lecture halls, bookshops, cafeterias and restrooms. There are underground parking facilities.

There are seven museums in one at the Louvre. It generally takes several days to tour the Louvre because it is so large. The underground facilities have more space for organized displays of the Lurvre's works and collections.

About two-thirds of what can be seen in the Louvre's department of painting is of the French School. Nicolas Poissin was of 17th Century classicism. He spent much of his life in Rome where drawing inspiration from ancient Greek and Roman Art and Renaissance painting he sought to perfect landscapes.

Claude Lorrain, another Baroque painter, created scenes of peasant life of the La Nain brothers.

Jean Antoine Watteau's paintings such as the Embarkation for the Island of Cythera are from the more delicate world of 18th Century Rococo Art. They are noted for their exquisite, dreamlike color, the elegance of Watteau's figures in graceful poses of dance and pantomime and his representation of pastoral bliss tinged with melancholy.

Jean Honore Fragonard, another well known French Rococo painter exhibited in the Louvre, dealt wittily with the theme of love and dalliance, setting his figures in luxuriant bowers. In a different vein, works by the 18th Century artist Jean Baptiste Greuze were admired in his day for their moral qualities. They strike the modern viewer as melodramatic and sentimental.

The most spectacular of the French school are on view in the vast Mallieu and Daru rooms, which contain the museum's largest paintings. There is the grand Coronation Ceremony of Napoleon by Jacques Louis David, Napoleon's official painter and one of the most important artistic figures of his time. He is associated with the Neoclassical style, which stressed a luminous precision, edifying grandeur, and a return to forms based on classical Greek art.

There is Theodore Gericault's Raft of the Medusa (1818-1819), a major work in the Romantic style, depicting castaways from a contemporary shipwreck. Liberty at the Barricades (1830) and another expressionistic painting were painted by Eugene Delacroix.

The Louvre has a rich selection of Italian Renaissance art which brings some of the Italian refinement into his own country, in particular by importing Italian artists. Leonardo da Vinci brought a number of his paintings with him to

France, which included the <u>Mona Lisa</u>, which became very famous. Raphael was another important artist, who has thirteen paintings in the Louvre.

Peter Paul Rubens has twenty-one paintings in the Louvre which are episodes from Marie's life in an allegorical form that appears tiresomely inflated today. The real quality of the Northern European schools is apparent in the smaller paintings like those of the Renaissance artists Jan van Eyck (The <u>Madonna of Chancellor Rolin</u>), Rogier van der Weyden (The <u>Brogue Triptych</u>) Hieronymus Bosch (The <u>Ship of Fools</u>), Han Holbein, the Younger (<u>Erusmus of Rotterdam</u>) and Pieter Brueghel in the 17th Century, artist Jan Vermeer (<u>The Lace-maker</u>) and in Rubens' less official paintings.

Venus de Milo is a well known sculpture at the Louvre. The collection also includes the charming Rampin head from the sixth century B.C. There are many famous sculptures in the Louvre in Paris, France. The Louvre has the works of many painters, sculptors, illustrators and decorators.

# FIFTY-FIVE

## *UNLOCKING THE GENETIC CODE*

In 1866 Gregor Mendel, an Austrian botanist, published a treatise, based on his experiments in crossbreeding pea plants, that defined the classical laws of genetics. A few years later a Swiss scientist, Friedrich Miescher made another momentous discovery when he extracted from trout sperm cells a substance believed to be instrumental in heredity.

It was not until 1953 that two Cambridge University researchers, Francis Crick and James Watson, opened a new era in biology by describing the chemical structure of that substance now known as deoxyribonucleic acid or DNA.

Within the past decades an unprecedented explosion of knowledge in genetics and molecular biology has dwarfed all the achievements of the past. A prominent scientist said, "We have learned more in the last few years than in the previous 2,000 years combined. And, in the next few years, we will have learned at least that much more."

This knowledge has transformed genetics from a descriptive science to an applied technology, has launched a billion-dollar industry, and promises to revolutionize the practice of medicine and the business of agriculture.

Genetics begins with DNA, an immensely long, spiraling molecule found in the nucleus of all living cells. Its basic structure is the now familiar double helix, usually pictured as two parallel strands, runged like a ladder and twisted like a ribbon. Each strand consists of four chemical bases – guanine, adenine, thymine and cytosine – repeated in a vast array of sequences throughout the length of the molecule. The four bases pair off between strands in an exclusive manner. Thus, the sequencing of one strand predicts and determines that of its opposite.

The nucleus of each of our cells contains all of the genetic instructions necessary to form a complete person – some three billion DNA base pairs. Fully unraveled, the DNA in a single cell would form a molecular chain some six feet long – a bit more than the average height of a male adult. Within the nucleus all this material is packed into a series of mocroscopic structures called chromosomes. In humans, each cell nucleus carries 23 pairs of chromosomes – one set provided by each parent, or 46 in all.

Chromosomes are actually tightly coiled bundles of genes which are discrete packets of DNA ranging in size from several hundred to several thousand base pairs. These genes are the fundamental units of heredity and their distinctive codes, or base sequences, provide the blueprint for all of our inborn traits. Some chromosomes come in matched sets. There are maternal and paternal versions of each gene. Altogether, some 50,000 to 100,000 gene pairs make up the human genome – the sum total of an individual's biological endowment.

Chromosomes have been observed through microscopes. Scientists have gained the ability to isolate, analyze and

manipulate individual genes. In the late 1960s and 1970s researchers found that certain bacterial enzymes could serve as biochemical "scissors" to slice the DNA molecule at specific locations. Released into a sample of whole DNA, an army of restriction enzymes will quickly reduce the genetic text to a pool of relatively short chapters.

With the help of another family of enzymes called DNA ligases, the fragments can be recombined and completely sealed so that no sign of the original cut remains. Since the basic molecular structure of all DNA is compatible, regardless of species, an endless variety of hybrid genes or gene fragments can be spliced together in this way.

A mass production of genes and gene products is the cornerstone of the new biotechnology industry, whose rapid growth has been featured prominently in the financial news of recent years. Approximately 300 biotechnology firms have sprung up around the United States and they are busily churning out products – most still experimental – that run the gamut from hardier strains of tobacco plants to new weapons in the war on cancer.

Most of the interest and excitement focuses on the medical uses of genetic engineering. Diagnostic probes – cloned fragments of DNA that are radioactively labeled or otherwise tagged so they can be traced in the body – have been developed for sniffing out elusive viral and bacterial diseases.

Today with the help of recombinant DNA probes, geneticists can test for the actual presence of a few genetic defects and they are closing in on many more. DNA researchers have devised several ingenious methods for employing probes. If a gene responsible for a disease is known and a specific coding error has been identified, it is a relatively simple matter for scientists to assemble a complementary, single-stranded DNA fragment that will see out and stick to the defect, indicating its presence. This probe – or clones versions of it – can then be used to screen anyone suspected of having or carrying the disease, with extremely accurate results.

Our DNA traits determine how our cells grow and respond to our environment. Each cell has a specific purpose and function. We need to continue to learn all we can about genes, chromosomes and our DNA. Unlocking the genetic code will help us understand the use of our genes and chromosomes.

# FIFTY-SIX

## *THE SCIENCE OF DREAMS*

Since man's beginnings dreams have occurred in man's sleep. Within recent years science has been able to provide a more comprehensive awareness for the reason we dream. Investigators have been able to determine the amount, frequency and content of dreams. During 20% of a night's sleep a person dreams. The dream state may help ensure the survival of the species and may be essential for mental health and physical well-being.

The ancients sensed that dreams were in some way linked to man's destiny. Before records were kept the myths of savage or primitive man perpetuated the belief that dreams were visits from departed souls. As soon as man could write he attempted to interpret dreams.

Among the first written documents is an Egyptian papyrus of dream interpretations from the Twelfth Dynasty (1991-1786 B.C.). the Greeks, Romans and Hebrews also believed in the importance of dreams. One theologian suggested that the three Magi who searched for the Christ child were priests of an Eastern cult skilled in dream interpretation.

But with monotheism came a strong reaction to the search for fateful signs in dreams. Christianity placed the will of God above the prophet's efforts to discern the future in dreams. For centuries respectable interest in dreams languished.

In the mid 19th Century progress made in the physical sciences suggested a series of mechanistic experiments to a few investigators. In one study sleepers were tickled with feathers, splashed with water and singed with candles all to show that dreams are caused by external factors.

Sigmund Freud made a study of dreams. In 1897 Freud undertook his own psychoanalysis which was an unsparing, detached and daring exploration of his hidden self. Freud suggested that there was beneath the conscious mind a layer of largely infantile and sexual emotions which he named the unconscious. At night, he explained, the conscious mind concentrates on the desire to sleep, to rest the body. At the same time the unconscious urgently demands release of its deep-seated drives. The dream represents that release, but it is a modified solution, a compromise between the need of the unconscious mind for full-scale gratification and the need of the body for rest.

In Sigmund Freud's own words the unconscious mind wishes to don disguises in order to creep past the dozing censors on the conscious mind. Symbolically transformed, wishes are expressed in dreams. After a time the unconscious is satisfied and the dream ends. Occasionally, however, the symbolic disguises are so thin that the censors are roused and the sleeper awakens, the victim of a nightmare.

Freud's interpretation of dreams fitted in with his explanation of neurotic behavior. Neuroses, he suggested, are caused by repression. That is, by the barring of disturbing material from consciousness – and exploring dreams is the best way for the psychoanalytically trained doctor to uncover the repressed self.

These ideas irrevocably changed man's ways of looking at himself and his dreams. Never again would dreams be dismissed solely as the product of a damp nightshirt or a highly seasoned meal. Twentieth Century psychology revived the ancient interest in dreams and successive generations of post-Freudians undertook to elaborate or alter Freud's original insights.

The greatest step forward in dream research, however, came not from psychology but from physiology. Beginning in the early 1930s Dr. Nathaniel Kleitman, a professor of physiology at the University of Chicago, devoted long hours to investigations of the physical processes of sleep. The subject had been curiously neglected. Sleep, a third of human life, was scarcely better understood than dreams.

Kleitman studied the "lost" eight hours of sleep and in the course of his experiments made the discoveries that may finally put an end to the centuries of speculation about dreams and dreaming. Kleitman discovered that babies made rapid eye movements. Their eyes continued to flutter beneath their closed lids. In time it was discovered that most sleepers tend to make eye movements when they sleep.

The hardest of all myths to shake has been the conviction of many people that they "just don't dream." The EEG and REM indicators tell researchers that the average adult – even assuming a below-the-norm quota of three dreams a night – is still producing over a thousand dreams a year. The great majority of these certainly are not recalled at all. Many others are remembered only in fragments.

The people who describe themselves as "good dreamers" are, obviously, just really "good rememberers." But why some people are good and others poor at remembering dreams is unclear. It is well known among psychiatrists that their patients' ability to recall dreams increases with therapy. But even these people, who are, in Dr. Ernest G. Schachtel's phrase, "sensitized to awareness," find it difficult or impossible to counteract the powerful tendency to forget.

Why are dreams forgotten? Wolpert and Trasman studied the transient nature of dreams. They found that the ability to recall a dream is a function of the "age" of the dream. Volunteers awakened during REM and dream periods produced richly detailed and complete narratives of their dream. Dreams may allow a person to release and exercise some of the mental tensions – aggression, fear, anxiety, anger and so on – that build up during a normal working day. In a sense, dreaming can be thought of as "thinking about the unthinkable" and the dream cycle can be viewed as a regular mechanism for clearing the mind of unfinished daytime business.

Dreaming is a normal experience when a person is sleeping. We illusinate while we dream. Dreaming is a subconscious experience. Some desires are experienced in our dreams.